SERGEY AVETISYAN

Nightlife Cities

the night-time economy

This book was professionally typeset on Reedsy.
Find out more at reedsy.com

For city science lovers.

Contents

Preface   iii

I   Part One

1   Backstory vibes   3
2   Nightlife   7
3   Origins of term   11
4   Assemblage   14
5   Planning's role   16
6   Deindustrialization   19

II   Part Two

7   Economics   27
8   Media forms   32
9   Wine and bear   35
10   Development   37

III   Part Three

11   Late-night   43
12   Alcohol   46
13   Maps   49
14   Culture   54

15 Transport   56

IV   Part Four

16 Party cities   61
17 The city that never sleeps   68
18 Back to the island   71
19 The party never ends   76
20 Most fashionable city   79

V   Part Five

21 Back to the features   85
22 Regulation   87
23 Municipal policy   90
24 Good night   93

Notes   96
About the Author   104

Preface

Every city science lover knows that cities are essential, because of the clustering force, cities and regions have become the actual engines of economic growth. The physicist Richard Feynman supposedly once said: *"if you think you understand quantum mechanics, you don't understand quantum mechanics."* I feel the same about the way *night-time economy*: otherwise, if we think we understand urban economics without night-time economy, we don't understand the urban economy. The night-time economy is increasingly being recognised as a driver of economic growth.

Cities can increase their productivity by adopting measures that regulate and diversify the array of social and economic activities that take place during the night. The night-time economy is a source of employment and additional revenue for local governments.

This book was written in a relaxed, journalistic style, it offers useful, practical tips from a wide range of leading scientists and experts on how to get on better in the modern urban life, particularly in a night-time. This *Nightlife Cities* is set out in five sections. The first three sections deal with different theoretical scenarios that occur in all countries. The last two section deals with practical notes that help in navigating such development scenarios.

Cities always remains energetic, even during the day. Yet a different form of vigor wave hits the city when the night dawns upon it. The nightclubs throng with the party animals, amazing cocktails line up the bar deck, and hands can be seen raised up in the air. Even the statues and buildings become "lit" in the night. But clubbing and partying are not the only things people enjoy cities nightlife. It is a chance again to think about the economy.

A lot of people around the world type their interest to "night-time economy", "jazz club" and "vacation" into Google.

In 2006, Google released Google Trends, a public tool that the research community can use to study anonymous and aggregate search data. That is how I found charts everything I will reported in this book. It is plausible that important and interesting facts about the night-time economy could be found here or in other data sets by data scientists, urban experts or data lovers.

I

Part One

"No one looks back on their life and remembers the nights they got plenty of sleep."

-Unknown-

1

Backstory vibes

What happens with the economy when the economists are sleeping? When the clock strikes and the lights go out, some of the world's most iconic cities come alive. Whisky bars, jazz clubs, pubs, and spectacular cabarets are only a few of the main attractions, and visitors will have no trouble finding after-hours entertainment. Why should we care about the night-time economy? It excites me to have come across an idea for night time, that will — inspire me to write about the nightlife of cities and the night-time economy. The concept for *Nightlife Cities* was born at 11:11 pm[1] a little while back while reading Umberto Eco's *"The Role Of The Reader"* (*"Lector In Fabula"*)[2] I've learned a lesson over the last couple of years: reading a book sparks valuable daydreaming and brainstorming. A couple of weeks ago, I read some articles *"Writing the city spatially"*) that convinced me to read more, mostly by finding *"hidden minutes"* during the day.[3] Before I started Jane Jacobs' book, I finished Steven Pinker's *"The Blank Slate"* by committing to reading at least one/two chapter every single night before bed. No matter how late my other activities - productive (university work, research, socializing) or otherwise (online video, articles about economics or sports) — kept me up, I'd read at least one/two chapter. So with *"creative class,"* I began to bring the book with me on the bus and pick it up at home in the middle of the day.[4] The first goal is being accomplished as I'm reading many more pages per day. But I didn't expect the side benefit: my mind wanders when I read, and it wanders to perfect places. Places like an old friend I want to communicate with, a high priority to-do I forgot about, or an idea for a new book. My mind doesn't wander like this when I'm on a light day usually.

My attention indeed strays, but it strays based on stimuli in front of my eyes, not in the back of my mind, and these afternoon-delivered diversions are usually not a high priority. This realization seems essential. We all know that it's good to read, but I'm starting to understand better why. I love the *#cityscience* the way I love night-time. People are flawed, they have a weakness, they fail, and they harm one another, but we're still better off with people in our lives. The *City* is flawed, it has a weakness, it sometimes fails to achieve its original purpose of creating a connection, and it can harm us by making information abundant but truth unclear. Anyway, we're still better off with the *Urban* in our lives.

Nightlife cities concept is less and less something that we can choose to avoid or incorporate into our lives only by choice. It's becoming a part of humanity itself, a central building block of society the same way people and ideas are building blocks of society. To contend with our flawed understanding, we have always discussed city development in ways that help us understand and improve it. In the modern age, we must include the night-time economy in the discussions we have about politics, economics, psychology, romance, and everything else. My love for *cities' night-time* is just like my love for the *#CityScience:* it's about people and their variety. Cities are humanity's habitat.

They're not our only habitat, but they support our species in all its forms, often with different forms side by side, better than any other environment. In *Death and Life of Great American Cities,* Jane Jacobs quotes Harvard professor Paul J. Tillich on how cities' diversity affects the people who live in them: *By its nature, the big cities provide what otherwise could be given only travelling; namely, the strange. Since the peculiar leads to questions and undermines familiar tradition, it elevates reason to ultimate significance.*

The big city is devoted to pieces, each of which is observed, purged, and equalized. The mystery of the strange and the critical rationality of citizen are both removed from the city. This book aims to summarize the main results of existing literature on the night-time economy and present cities unified manner. For this purpose, I have two goals in this book: to inform the reader about advances in our scientific understanding of night-time economy and to show how much scientific knowledge can help us make the science of our politics. Second give information about some concepts in assemblage urbanism, leisure industry, and urban development. A fundamental posit of the book is that the *Nightlife Cities* is just the latest trend catchphrase capturing a spectrum of flexible urban economy transformation and arrangements that have existed before in one form or another. The purpose of this book is to explain concisely to a non-specialist readership what is meant by the *"the night-time economy,"* how it operates and what implications it poses for the workers and businesses that work within its confines, and what issues it raises for the broader economy and policymakers. Creating a safe, vibrant and well-balanced evening and night-time offer is a challenge. Still, with fantastic growth potential, more and more local partnerships are finding unique and innovative ways to approach the task. Effective management of a place's evening and night-time economy is quickly becoming a priority in the majority of locations across Europe. People are starting realizing that sustainable economic prosperity can only be achieved by taking a holistic approach to the management of a place and understanding our town and city centres don't have to close at 6 pm.

5

It's important to know what people are searching for and why. Google Trends is a tool that reveals trending search queries and shows how popular different keyword phrases are over time.

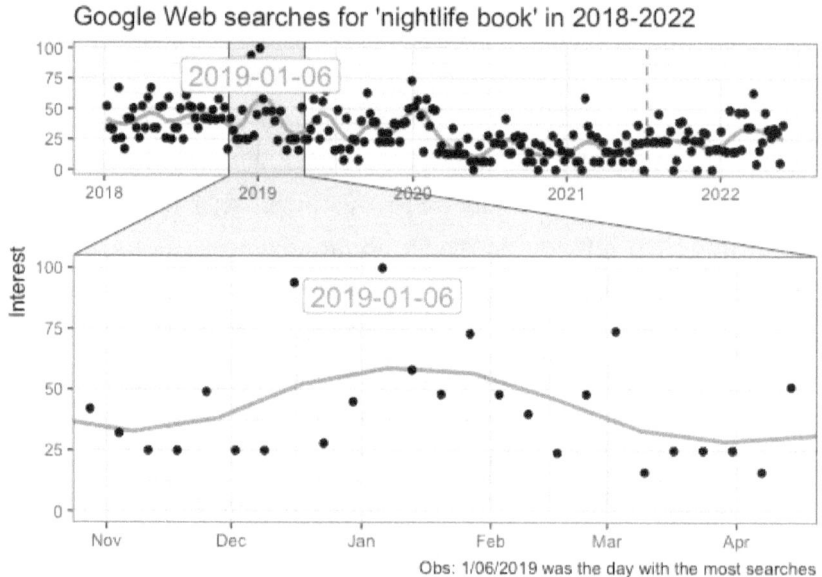

Obs: 1/06/2019 was the day with the most searches

Google Searches for "Nightlife book."

2

Nightlife

One part of the night-time economy is the city's nightlife. The rise of the night-time economy —portrayed by leisure zones, cheap alcohol deals, and extended drinking hours—have created urban spatial hotspots of reported brutality and antisocial behaviour. To the contrary, the night-time economy represents the development of city centers. The night-time economy is a concept that refers to the range of leisure activities and experiences associated with patterns of collective night-time socializing and entertainment, including drinking, eating and creative practice. The *Night-Time Economic* is an increasingly important subject of interest to researchers, policymakers, private business and public agencies, and the media and the wider community[5]. Throughout history, towns and cities have had some manifestation of an *"economy"* that operates in the evening and night. In ancient times people traded objects and services beyond the end of the commonly understood *"working day."* In Asia, night markets selling domestic goods, medicines, and food have existed for thousands of years.

Anyway, in the 21st-century leisure or *"post-industrial"* age, the evening and night's transactional nature has appeared to grow in importance to towns and cities' functioning. So while perhaps not the same content of economic contribution as an activity during the daytime, what happens *"after dark"* has become much more significant and perhaps visible for a range of reasons which we set out below. This is particularly true in Western and Western-influenced nations, where some have had a difficult relationship with the *"night,"* instinctively seen as something to be feared, avoided and regulated. The first conceptualization and research into the *"night-time economy,"* as it quickly became known, appeared in the early 1990s when a small number of cultural and urban theorists identified that European town and city centers, after dark, had their own unique qualities. While these qualities did not entirely separate them from the *"day-time,"* it was clear they produced certain distinct sociological phenomena and raised issues different from those that drove urban governance and city management during the day. These early studies focused on the liberating, consumer-oriented and urban planning aspects of the night-time industry. More broadly, the nighttime economy is a striking manifestation of the intricate and dynamic relationship between the social, cultural and material economies of cities with an emphasis on leisure and lifestyle.[6]

The night-time economy concept has gained increasing currency since the 1990s in seeking to encapsulate changes to the organization and practice of after-dark life, especially in urban settings. Different rhythms of work and leisure, and of the uses of city spaces, as well as the increased economic significance of the services sector (especially of tourism), has promoted the idea of a 24-hour city with more fluid and diverse leisure pursuits, particularly of a *"cultural-intellectual"* nature.[7] The development and management of the night-time economy is one of the most important issues facing cities worldwide. It needs to be addressed in a range of different contemporary urban locations across countries, including all state capitals and, less obviously, in regional centres. The night-time economy can deliver great cultural, social and economic benefits to a lot of cities. Anyway, it may have major costs in terms of social disruption and disputes, assaults and serious injuries that drain public criminal justice and health resources. Therefore, developing and managing the night-time economy is a key imperative for any city looking to effectively integrate the various dimensions of working, domestic and leisure life. Nightlife is a collective term for entertainment that is available and generally more popular from the late evening into the morning's early hours. It includes pubs, bars, night-clubs, parties, live music, concerts, cabarets and shows. These venues often require a cover charge for admission. Nightlife entertainment is often more adult-oriented than daytime entertainment. People who prefer to be active during the night-time are called night owls. In planning, the evening economy describes economic activity taking place in the evening after many people finish daytime employment or formal education, such as eating and drinking, entertainment, and nightlife (which may be described by the related term nighttime economy). The evening economy includes activities, but is not limited to:

- Eating out - *restaurants, cafés, takeaways,*
- Drinking - *pubs and bars,*
- Culture and entertainment - *cinemas, live music and comedy events, ten pin bowling, ice skating,*
- Sport - *spectator sports including football, rugby and greyhound racing often take place in the evening, especially during Mondays to Fridays,*
- Healthcare, police and firefighting.

Benefits and drawbacks, benefits of a significant evening economy can include:

- Recreation for people, which is often welcome after finishing work for the day,

- Increased employment due to local spending,
- Reduced social exclusion and increased vitality in towns.

The drawbacks can include:

- Noise pollution,
- Crime and/or anti-*social behaviour, particularly where alcohol is involved,*
- Traffic congestion.

3

Origins of term

Nightlife has been a vibrant area of research for sociologists. Nightlife establishments including pubs, bars, and night-clubs function as third places, according to Ray Oldenburg in *"The Great Good Place."*[8] As a phrase for describing the alcohol and leisure industry in the night-time city, the term *"night-time economy"* has its origins in the work of the academics associated with Charles Landry's creative cities research organization Comedia. Franco Bianchini, one of the academics involved in Comedia at the time, dated the term to 1987, and the Italian politician Renato Nicolini, who had been responsible for a series of cultural festivals, including night-time activities, in Rome called *"L'Estate Romana"* between 1977 and 1985.[9] This would fit with academic publications: the phrase does not appear in the 1986 book on British cultural policy Saturday Night or Sunday Morning[10] but is used in a 1990 article on cities and cultural planning by John Montgomery.[11] From this, it is clear that the night-time economy first gained currency in planning circles. Specifically, the term's circulation was associated with groups such as *Comedia's attempts* to encourage the deregulation and development of the alcohol and leisure industry at night in both political and academic fields[12]. As Bianchini states: *"In the case of*

11

important regional cities the night-time could be used to maximize access to urban facilities from a wide catchment area. People from that area, many of whom are working in the day- time, may need longer opening hours to access facilities. More generally, there is the opportunity of 'doubling' the city's economy, starting perhaps from entertainment but then widening into other areas."[13]

It is the opportunity to *"double"* the city's economy, by doubling the period of time by which city centres are productive, that is at the heart of the argument for a night-time economy raised by Bianchini and others. Furthermore, this phrase's formulation is connected to the discursive power of the word *"economy"*(rather than alternatives such as or night-time culture), particularly as this attempt to promote the urban night as a source of cultural production occurred during the recovery from the early 1990s recession in the UK.

Google Trends contains two extremely helpful sections: "Related topics" and "Related queries.

Graph below shows google trends queries of jazz club.

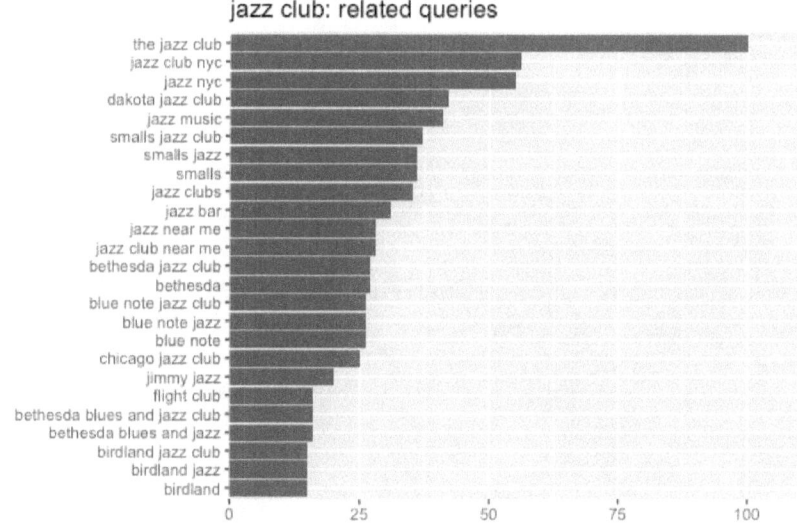

jazz club: related queries

4

Assemblage

The assemblage was first introduced by Deleuze and Guattari, who used the term agencement (French for *assemblage*) to highlight the way in which human and non-human components, including actors, discursive elements (statements, plans, and policies) and materials (nature, infrastructure, etc.), are linked in a rhizomatic network. Assemblage components *"from near and far"* made up of *"fixed and mobile expertise and regulations"* are always in the process of "coming together (territorialization), just as always also potentially pulling apart (deterritorialization)".* In this light, an assemblage describes the constellation's dynamic process in which a composition of heterogeneous elements forms a provisional socioeconomic relation but is always subject to change.

In urban studies, the assemblage is employed in large loosely related bodies of work that focus on relational thinking. These studies include actor-network theory (ANT), non-representational thinking, *"new materialist"* geographies, and politics of knowledge. After Latour's book Reassembling the Social that introduces the ANT, relational thinking has attracted growing attention in urban studies. The different human and non-human elements are entangled in assemblage as they have been frequently demonstrated.

However, we can still roughly discern two priorities through *"the things"* studies follow: those that follow material elements and those that follow discursive elements. What are the causes of the relative underdevelopment of urban nightlife in Britain? Some important factors were highlighted by Comedia's Out of Hours study (1989±91). One key problem was that there simply was not enough to do at night in some town and city centres.

Another was the peculiarity of pub culture: predominantly male and youth-orientated, a culture of heavy drinking behind opaque glass windows, with little communication between the pub and the street. Equally discussed were the issues of the monofunctionality of town and city centres, dominated by shops and offices, and of the unfriendliness to pedestrians of places designed and planned for the motor car: town and city centres dominated by ugly and dangerous inner ring roads, underpasses and multistory car parks.[14]

According to Heath, at the end of the twentieth century, our cities face a multitude of problems both of a spatial and functional nature. One of the key issues to be addressed is the limited time—9 a.m. to 5 p.m. — during which we utilize the facilities and opportunities that the city centre has to offer.[15] The Twenty-four Hour City concept is a relatively recent approach of combining a series of wide-ranging initiatives to tackle this problem by revitalizing and creating safer city centres. This approach aims to attract a wide range of groups back into the city both to use the services and facilities that it has to offer and as residents. Heath's approach will explore the key issues of the Twenty-four Hour City concept and examine the important initiatives that have been adopted in various cities in the UK.

5

Planning's role

James Rouse[16] is a master planner, *"credited variously, if not always accurately, with coining the term urban renewal."* Rouse spoke out against sprawl, deeming it anti-human, and centered his attention on bringing people back into the city by creating festival marketplaces. *"Rousification"* became one of the precedents for the re-use of post-industrial localities for cultural purposes, that has been reproduced worldwide. The *"standard"* festival marketplace includes local involvement in creating a safe and trendy attraction as a catalyst for other development. It has typical features of restaurants, speciality retail, nightlife, and entertainment. These features form the *"festivalisation."*[17]

Planning has a key role to play in ensuring a thriving night-time economy. For a start, having a pub, club, or other cultural venue designated as an asset of community value would help protect the venue's use from future development. The planning system is key to the promotion of sustainable leisure economies. At a central level, national planning policy must reinforce the leisure economy's cultural and economic value. The local planning framework must:

• Translate the leisure strategy into practical planning policy.

- Identify the zones for the development of leisure facilities.
- Promulgate policies to encourage such development.
- Identify leisure assets of value to the community.
- Protect such assets against loss or threats from incompatible development.

In recent times, planning policy has encouraged the development of residential uses in town and city centres. This is a positive trend. Anyway, leisure uses are now being lost to residential development, and new residential users are pressurizing authorities into preventing new leisure uses or curtailing the rights of established uses. Planning authorities have a key role in ensuring that an appropriate balance is maintained between the development of residential uses, the protection of established leisure uses and the development of new leisure uses.

Our towns and cities' success depends on one group's needs, not being permitted to predominate over another's needs. In the case of new residential uses, the planning system can assist by effective spatial planning. Residential uses are not planned next to late-night facilities, requiring construction measures to minimize nuisance or requiring developers to waive rights to complain of the nuisance.

Urbanism was at the heart of the revolution of US forms of leisure. As the developing economies shifted from agriculture to industry in the nineteenth century, scores of young women and men moved into the rapidly growing city to take advantage of new employment opportunities.

These people important not only for a new type of economy and work practice but also a new form of sociality and urban living. The bars and theatres that developed were akin to melting pots where people ordinarily separated by class, or social mores could come together.

Somers places these venues within the context of new forms of community. Typically young and single, those who came to the burgeoning cities lived alone in boarding houses and hostels and sought new recreation and intimacy forms.[18] Away from the traditional family structure and from the homogeneous world of rural communities, the city offered an immense array of opportunities to meet and mingle with others, be those strangers, new friends or lovers. In turn, new forms of sociality came to exist, and more importantly, for the argument here, new social spaces where such meetings could occur.

This is, of course, a familiar narrative of city life. According to Bauman, whatever the changes to the physical form, economy and way of life in cities, *"one feature has remained constant: cities are spaces where strangers stay and move close to one another."*

Britain's industrialized urban centres emerged much earlier than those in the USA. Still, a comparable theme can be seen in how the city is often represented as a cornucopia of new pleasures and opportunities awaiting the newcomer. Whether they are fresh from education or from smaller towns, single people have long been seen as the vanguard of city life. They are typically represented as driving the night-time city, its shape, character, and the leisure opportunities it offers.

Local administration and the nightlife economy commonly try to enhance experienced safety through increased surveillance and policing of – what is widely regarded as – incivilities and antisocial behaviours. Prevention of fear is key to development strategies configured around pleasure and consumption; it is widely agreed that safe and enjoyable spaces will attract more consumers and spending.[19]

6

Deindustrialization

The Night-Time Economic is an increasingly important subject of interest to researchers. As this book attests, policymakers, private business and public agencies, and the media and the wider community. Throughout history, towns and cities have had some manifestation of an *"economy"* that operates in the evening and at night. So, people traded objects and services beyond the end of the commonly understood *"working day"*. In Asia, night markets selling domestic goods, medicines, and food have existed for thousands of years. Anyway, in the 21st-century leisure or *"post-industrial"* age, the evening and night's transactional nature has appeared to grow in importance to towns and cities' functioning. So while perhaps not the same content of economic contribution as an activity during the day- time, what happens *"after dark"* has become much more significant and perhaps visible for a range of reasons which we set out below. This is particularly true in Western and Western-influenced nations, where some have had a difficult relationship with the *"night,"* instinctively seen as something to be feared, avoided and regulated. The conceptualisation and research into the *"night-time economy,"* as it quickly became known, appeared in the early 1990s when a small number of cultural and urban theorists identified that European town and city centres, after dark, had their own unique qualities. While these qualities did not entirely separate them from the *"day-time,"* it was clear they produced certain distinct sociological phenomena and raised issues different from those that drove urban governance and city management during the day. These early studies focused on the liberating, consumer-oriented and urban planning aspects of the NTE.

However, since the late 1990s, and partly in reaction to the pro-NTE-liberalisation agenda influenced by these early studies, there has been a considerable inquiry into the NTE by academics from sociological, criminological and health backgrounds, often focusing on the costs, negative externalities or 'negative impacts associated with activity after dark. The Night-Time Economic (NTE) is an increasingly important subject of interest to researchers, policymakers, private business and public agencies, and the media and the wider community. Throughout history, towns and cities have had some manifestation of an *"economy"* that operates in the evening and at night. In Ancient Greece (and probably before) people traded objects and services beyond the end of the commonly understood *"working day."* In Asia, night markets selling domestic goods, medicines, and food have existed for thousands of years. Anyway, in the 21st-century leisure or *"post-industrial"* age, the evening and night's transactional nature has appeared to grow in importance to towns and cities' functioning. So while perhaps not the same content of economic contribution as an activity during the daytime, what happens *"after dark"* has become much more significant and perhaps visible for a range of reasons which we set out below. This is particularly true in Western and Western-influenced nations, where some have had a difficult relationship with the *"night"* instinctively seen as something to be feared, avoided and regulated.

The first conceptualization and research into the *"night-time economy,"* as it quickly became known, appeared in the early 1990s when a small number of cultural and urban theorists identified that European town and city centres, after dark, had their own unique qualities. While these qualities did not entirely separate them from the "day-time" it was clear they produced certain distinct sociological phenomenon and raised issues different to those that drove urban governance and city management during the day. These early studies focused on the liberating, consumer-oriented and urban planning aspects of the NTE. Anyway, since the late 1990s, and partly in reaction to the pro - NTE - liberalisation agenda influenced by these early studies, there has been a considerable inquiry into the NTE by academics from sociological, criminological and health backgrounds, often focusing on the costs, negative externalities or negative impacts associated with activity after dark. The 1980s saw the re-emergence of a concern with city centres as focal points for, and as symbolic of, a specifically urban way of life seemingly eroded in the 1970s. Although social justice and local democracy questions remained, these new concerns pushed cultural questions to the fore. This shift's context was complex, but we can pick out what we would consider being the main features.

The first aspect is the deindustrialization of older industrial areas which left large portions of older city centres derelict with the con-sequent shattering of local and regional identity brought on by this economic crisis and which this dereliction powerfully symbolized.

Whole cities and regions that had grown up around an industrial production rooted in place and central to forming the local popula-tion's working and living patterns now found themselves radically undermined. This was to do not only with the devastating effects of long-term structural unemployment but with a wider sense of loss of purpose; of identity. In the industrial cities of Northern England, Scotland, Northern France, the Ruhr, The Nether- lands, a collective identity crisis could be perceived in the early 1980s. Ugly grim cities they may have been, but formerly they produced, they made for the world. Now they were just ugly and grim.

21

The second aspect is the revalorisation of city centre sites in the development boom, which began in the late 1970s, and early 1980s. Hanging on in many cities in the mid-1970s the central business districts (CBDs) represented a fixed capital that companies were extremely reluctant to write off. This was not just in terms of buildings but also of the land.[20] The rise of footloose capital in the context of 1970s restructuring meant that investment capital was available to recoup the 'true' value of the CBD. Crucial to this strategy was a reinvention or re-emphasis on the prestige of centrality. New city centre offices, as well as residential and leisure developments, emphasized this centrality through the promotion of the unique value of urbanity signs and images of urban living that had atrophied in the 1960s and 1970s or had acquired purely negative connotations. This revalorisation was not just aimed at the CBD. In the new regeneration models of the North American developers, those areas adjacent to the CBD were more than a bonus windfall, they were central to the regeneration package. Not just the real estate value but also the *cultural capital* represented by downtowns' were to be recouped by the developers recreating them as sites of a *"new urbanity"* centred around leisure, up-market consumption, and prestigious residential living intended to signal this *"new urbanity"* through echoes of the *"new bohemianism"* of 1970s pioneer gentrification.[21]

The third aspect is the emergence of city-to-city competitiveness at a national and supranational level. The management of the local image was deemed crucial in an increasingly globalized marketplace.

This image was tied to the cultural facilities and "vibrancy" of the city center. If deindustrialization was about the abstraction of production from a place, and if the *"post-industrial"* economies were about footloose service sector workers, then cities with a bad image would lose out. Unfortunately, the problem was that city authorities often had little knowledge of the cultural sector, which was moved from a peripheral to a central place in local policymaking in ways that often involved crass and heavy-handed opportunism. This caused tension within the cultural sector, as those working within the cultural field were faced with a whole new set of external demands and success indices. It also caused tensions within the local area as *"high culture"* was given precedence in funding programs. Also, it created tensions within the local polity as planners trained to deal with the city as a system of objective factors were faced with notions of urban cultures and spaces that few were equipped to deal with.[22]

The fourth aspect was the reorganization of city centres around consumption rather than production. If planners were faced with a new emphasis on urban culture and space, demanding approaches to regulation, the more immediate and powerful pressures for a retreat from regulation stemmed from the market often backed up with political expediency. In the 1980s the (unevenly) revalorised city centre emerged as a new landscape of buildings, enterprises and signs concerned with the organization and exploitation of consumption. This economy of consumption (distribution and marketing), unlike the economy of the production and exchange of goods (manufacturing and trade), had a much looser relationship to the local area. The big players in this new consumer economy were global. In their establishment, at the heart of the new city centre, they radically redrew the local and global boundaries in the city. It was not just that all city centres began to look the same but that the relation to place, to the local involvement in this globalised consumption, was made increasingly tenuous.

II

Part Two

"There is no night life in Spain. They stay up late but they get up late. That is not night life. That is delaying the day. Night life is when you get up with a hangover in the morning. Night life is when everybody says what the hell and you do not remember who paid the bill. Night life goes round and round and you look at the wall to make it stop. Night life comes out of a bottle and goes into a jar. If you think how much are the drinks it is not night life."

-Ernest Hemingway-

7

Economics

Nightlights could be a new way to measure economic growth. Economists at the Brown University in the US have a framework for estimating a country's gross domestic product (GDP) using satellite images of the area's nighttime lights. In their research paper, economists J Vernon Henderson, Adam Storeygard, and David N Weil say they don't envision the lights density data as a replacement for official numbers, but when added to existing data from agencies like the World Bank, the density of the lights can provide a better indicator of how these economies really are performing.[23]

According to J Vernon Henderson, Adam Storeygard, and David N Weil's article *"Measuring Economic Growth from Outer Spac"*, where they are developing a statistical framework to use satellite data on night lights to augment official income growth measures, approach for countries with poor national income accounts, the optimal estimate of growth is a composite with roughly equal weights on conventionally measured growth and growth predicted from lights. They estimates differ from official data by up to three percentage points annually. Using lights, empirical analyses of growth need no longer use countries as the unit of analysis; paper can measure sub- and supranational regions' growth.

For example, coastal areas in sub-Saharan Africa are growing slower than the hinterland.

The luminosity studies so far aim to examine the underlying relationship between nightlights and economic variables such as GDP growth, development and population. Sometimes, nightlights are used to create an index of development, a density ratio of human settlements, etc. On the other hand, Neural Networks is an alternative estimation method in the econometrics used for complex systems. These are the black box models which do not need giving an economic meaning to the estimated relationship.

Henderson et al., first review the literature of nightlights as a proxy measure in an economy, and second briefly mention concerning areas of *Neural Networks*[24] in econometrics. William Nordhaus of Yale University states that about 3,000 studies have used nightlights as a proxy of economic activities since 2000.

Chen and Nordhaus statistically examine how well nightlights can help researchers measure the countries' economic activities.[25] They find that satellite images are very useful in assessing the economic activities of cities and regions. They also note that traditional data sources are often far less reliable. The studies show that nightlights can be used as a proxy for many variables such as urbanization, city dynamics, population movements, economic growth, development indicator and

A neural network is a network or circuit of neurons or an artificial neural network composed of artificial neurons or nodes in a modern sense. Thus, a neural network is either a biological neural network, made up of real biological neurons or an artificial neural network, for solving artificial intelligence problems. The connections of the biological neuron are modelled as weights. A positive weight reflects an excitatory connection, while negative values mean inhibitory connections. All inputs are modified by weight and summed. This activity is referred to as a linear combination. Finally, an activation function controls the amplitude of the output.

Mellander et al. examine the correlation between population density and nightlights by using geocoded residential and industrial microdata of Sweden and radiance and saturated light emissions. They find a strong correlation to make nightlights a relatively good proxy for economics activities.[26]

Doll et al., based on the data of 11 European Union Countries and the United States, maps regional economic activity from nightlights satellite images.[27] They find that there is a strong positive relationship between the nightlight series and GDP across a range of spatial scale. Also, authors of World Bank, Bundervoet et al. (2015), estimated GDP growth rates and levels for 47 counties in Kenya and 30 districts in Rwanda by using satellite imagery.[28] Forbes examines whether there is a statistical correlation between GDP and nightlights data at Metropolitan Statistical Era (MSA) of Florida.

Forbes not only finds a strong correlation, but he also detects specific industries within each MSA, contributing to the variance of nightlights at the greatest amount.[29]

Ghosh et al., use the radiance-calibrated night- lights as a proxy measure of human well-being at both the national and subnational level. They review regressing the sum of lights intensity values for countries against their official GDP plus informal economy.[30] They create 36 overlapping groups of administrative units at different levels of economic development with ratios of the sum of light intensity to official GDP and GSP (Gross Sub-National Product) plus informal economy. The regression model calibrates the sum of lights intensity to the official GDP values or GSP plus informal economy for all 36 groups. They obtained R2 greater than 0.9 for all groups. Sutton et al., estimate GDP at the sub-national level for the countries, China, India, Turkey, and the United States. The study stays limited to estimate sub-national

GDP as a time series, although it provides beneficial instruments in the starting point[31]. Briefly, they use two different methods; the first one is aka summation of light intensity values. The second one is a spatial analytic approach using the lit area's areal extent and non-linear relationship between nightlights and population.[32]

After disaggregating the DMSP OLS according to sub-national administrative units, sub-national level lights integrations (first and second) are regressed against to sub-national level GDP values of corresponding countries including Turkey. The residuals from the regression models, which are divided into 5 quintiles, are used to create regional parameters. In order to predict sub-national GDP in 2000, they apply regional parameters derived from errors in 1992- 1993 data to the 2000 data.

However, Sutton argues that aka summation of light intensity suffers from night-lights' saturation in urban core centers. For example, R2 of the first simple model is 0.58 for Turkey. However, R2 increases dramatically to 0.95 in the second approach. They suppose that the reason for the improvement is due to the fact.[33]

Istanbul is a single giant city composing a large fraction of the GDP of its nation. Therefore, this simple model relatively fails to estimate without correcting DMSP OLS regarding areal lit. One of the most pronounced studies is conducted by Vernon Henderson, Adam Storeygard and David Weil from Brown University in 2009. In their study, the intensity of outer space lights, i.e. nightlights, emitted from the countries as an outcome of electricity consumption, is used to measure the true GDP of 188 countries over 17 years. In addition, they provide a long-term picture of differences in income of South and North Korea. For the first time, Henderson et al. use nightlights as a tool, more than a proxy, to correct GDP series of 188 countries.

Moreover, Pinkovskiy and Sala-i Martin use nightlights as a referee variable to compare national accounts GDP per capita to survey means in measuring true GDP of India and Angola[34]. The spirit of their study is very close to Henderson (et al.).

In both studies, the official GDP measurement errors are assumed to be uncorrelated with the errors resulting from physical conditions affecting luminosity record quality. This is the necessary assumption for our study, as well. Both Henderson and Pinkovskiy and Sala-i Martin benefit nightlights to correct miscalculated official GDP of some countries.[35] However, we use a different method to benefit nightlights as a tool to estimate national and sub-national level GDP due to the reasons mentioned earlier. The method we exploit is Neural Networks analysis. Kuan and White (1994) are the first ones giving the definitive introduction of Neural Network to the econometric literature.[36] Maasoumi applies Their theoretical approaches show that fourteen macroeconomic series would be well modelled with Neural Networks.[37]

Tkacz, with his colleges, examines whether the forecasting performance of financial and monetary variables for output growth can be improved using *Neural Networks*.[38] They find that neural network predicts GDP growth with fewer errors than its linear counterparts such as ARIMA. Feng and Zhang show the application of artificial neural network in forecasting economic growth.[39] They obtain a map of stimuli effect of various known and unknown variables over GDP growth via a combination of nonlinear functions. In addition, Sokolov-Mladenovic (et al.) predicts economic growth based on trade indicators with two different neural network algorithms.[40] Considering both the implementation of neural network in macroeconomic analysis and using nightlights as an indicator for economic activities, there are novel works of literature. Among many approaches, the combination of these two seems to create an accurate solution for the question and conditions specific to data in hand.

8

Media forms

On October 17, 2014, *The New York Times* published a lengthy article entitled *"In New York City, Sunday Night Is for Regulars."*[41] The report followed a well- established journalistic form, that of the night-time journey through a large city. The author/journalist ventured into the Manhattan night in order to discover the sorts of people who frequented places of night-time congregation and the varieties of behaviour in which they engaged. The article interviewed people patronizing late-night bars and restaurants, and found, in places and practices usually ignored in journalistic coverage of the city, vestiges of an older urbanity.

Nearly a century earlier, in the New York-based scandal magazine Broadway Brevities, a 13-part series of articles titled *"Nights in Fairyland"* followed a reporter as he visited the sites of late-night gatherings of gays and lesbians in Manhattan (Broadway Brevities 1924-1925). Most of these places were hidden from public view, in the backrooms of other establishments or concealed behind solid doors in basement hideaways. In the 2014 New York Times article, the urban night was treated as an uncharted, unknown world whose characters and rituals were perceived as sufficiently strange to warrant coverage in these highly narrativized journalistic treatments. Of the many differences between these two recounted journeys, a principal one has to do with how the night is imagined in relationship to social change. In 2014, those people encountered in the Manhattan night were, for the most part, familiar social types associated with the city's past and suspected of no longer inhabiting the city: the elderly of reduced means, the working class, and others who invoked an older, convivial New York as it existed before recent waves of gentrification.

In the "Nights in Fairyland" series of 1924-25, the night worlds discovered were, on the contrary, those of emerging communities, of behaviours or values deemed transgressive and novel in relation to a dominant moral order. Those media treatments of the night which we designate as exploratory have long moved between these divergent visions of the nocturnal city - between a view of the night as a memory- space, in which residual lifestyles and habits find refuge from the corrosive effects of changes associated with the day, and a vision of the night as the optimal time/space of experimentation and innovation.

These figures are condensed in Jim Jarmusch's film Only Lovers Left Alive (2013), whose vampire heroes are both archaic survivors of centuries-old histories and participants in the present-day settlement of hipster destinations like Detroit and Tangiers. This double sense of urban night worlds is captured, as well, in Dominique Kalifa's survey of 19th century journalistic and fictional journeys through the basfonds (the lower depths) of European cities like Paris.[42]

For Kalifa, the night spaces of criminality and bohemian lifestyle discovered (or invented) by the authors he studied functioned, on the one hand, as vestiges of medieval obscurity lingering in a city which was in the process of being transformed according to the principles of modern urban planning. At the same time, the immigrant and transient populations depicted as inhabiting these depths were, in important ways, distinctly new; they stood for a social heterogeneity which could easily be diagnosed as typical of emerging modernity. The media texts described above exemplify the exploratory mode by which media have engaged with the urban night. In this mode, the night is the time/space of a journey, typically organized as a series of encounters with people and places. Among the media forms in which this mode has been most common, we may point to documentary films which examine a city through the device of a voyage through its nightlife, such as the Canadian film *Montreal by Night* (dir. *Arthur Burrows, Jean Palardy 1947*) or the French film *Paris la nuit* (dir. *Jacques Baratier, Jean Val'ere 1960*). Another variant of this exploratory mode is the semi-pornographic urban expose, a journalistic form that employs the structure of the investigative journey to organize the presentation of the content of an exploitative and titillating character.[43]

9

Wine and bear

In recent years it has become common to associate late-night culture with alcohol and drinking.[44] Alcohol has most certainly played a central role in the night-time city. How- ever, the relationship between cities and consumer practices are mediated via an array of macro and micro-processes. Rather than having a direct causal link, the late-night city has emerged in the context of local and international forces about the economic, cultural and political. New consumer groups and subcultures have played an equally significant role, with these factors further 'constrained and enabled' about the everyday performance of race, age, class, sexuality and gender. Echoing this point, Latham argues that cities are more than just sites of consumption. They serve as backdrops through which different ways of inhabiting and *"doing"* the city are enabled.

The city's economic and commercial functions are fundamental to the development of the contemporary late-night city, but the ways it is inhabited, what it means and what people 'do' is far more than just a simple economic relation. As Bell has similarly argued, to focus excessively on economic factors results in ignoring the more *"mundane"* activities of sociality. In short, the city at night is every bit as complex –

and can be every bit as mundane as the city in the day-time.

Although the change from industrial to post-industrial capitalism is best understood as a rapid evolutionary process transforming a social and economic order based upon production to one based upon consumption, this process also indicates an accompanying shift from the problematic producer to the uncertain consumer. There is a wealth of evidence that violence is a significant by-product of *"rowdy and violent group drinking, the construction and projection of empowered masculine identity, and the symbolic rejection of respectable social values,"* all of which lie at the heart of the night-time economy. In England and Wales, 70 per cent of crime audits identified *'alcohol as an issue, particularly about public order'*, and the bulk of hot-spots were in areas containing high concentrations of licensed premises, with the number of incidents peaking between 9 p.m.and 3 a.m. on Friday nights/Saturday mornings and Saturday nights/ Sunday mornings. Although correlations do not account for causation, and the relationship between venue density/proliferation and associated violence and disorder is involved, the overwhelming evidence available from major cities and smaller urban centres alike is that increases in the number (and especially density) of licensed premises, their total capacities and terminal trading hours contribute to a rise in assaults and public order offences. In summary, when the activity levels of an intoxicated night-time consumer base increase, then, as one might expect, more crime and disorder will be generated in the streets and public spaces of our night-time leisure zones. However, violence, disease, anti-social behaviour, criminal damage, vandalism and noise are not contained exclusively within urban leisure zones. Still, they are manifest along dispersal routes as well as within domestic contexts.

10

Development

The *night-time economy* will be the inner potential for development. To feed and house people, we will have to create more on the same land. But cities don't have to grow higher and lower— into the sky or underground — they can also grow in the use of time. Exploring how to make more use of the evening and nighttime provides jobs, supports community cohesion and supports social inclusion. A growing city, one capable of meeting the needs of an increasing population of all ages, expands into the night. In London, the night-time economy is predicted to grow by £2bn from 2017 to 2026.

Melbourne, Australia's fastest-growing city, has more leisure and entertainment premises per capita within its city limits than any other city in the world. Austin, the self-proclaimed *"live music capital of the world,"* is also America's fastest-growing city, with over 1m inhabitants. Not only are these cities growing in size, but they are also making better use of their time — their evenings and night-times.

Spending on after dark dining rose 40-50 per cent last year, with Beijing and Shanghai leading way. Authorities nationwide have beefed up measures to develop the night-time economy, with steps to encourage post-dusk business activities and later closing hours at museums and art galleries.

The moves follow reports that China's economic growth slowed to 6.2 per cent year-on-year in the second quarter, its weakest pace in at least 27 years, with consumption contributing more than 60 per cent of GDP growth.

Some cities, including Beijing, Shanghai, Tianjin and Jinan, the capital of Shandong province, have recently rolled out measures to shore up the nighttime economy, also known as after-hours economic activity, with longer operating hours for public transport.

The Beijing Municipal Bureau of Commerce unveiled a string of policies last month to support the nighttime economy's growth and better meet demand for more high- quality, diversified and convenient consumption options. The moves include later closing hours at tourist spots, museums, sports grounds and art galleries. The city will extend the operating hours of several subway lines every Friday, Saturday and Sunday, and 25-night bus lines will operate more frequently in key areas. Seven new bus lines will also facilitate night travel for large residential communities in the city's north. So, there was a great deal of potential for different areas to promote nighttime business activities.

Local authorities have an important role to play. The most important thing is to ensure good planning and innovative development. They must give play to local strengths and create an enabling environment for consumers.

Zhao said the scope of the nighttime economy extended far beyond night markets.

The catering sector is only the starting point. There is still so much to explore in aspects of culture and tourism.

The authorities in Shanghai unveiled a list of cultural activities and tour routes on Thursday to boost the city's nighttime economy. The Municipal Culture and Tourism Bureau said 105 tourist spots, art galleries, museums and memorials across the city had taken measures to meet the growing demand for nighttime leisure activities from Shanghai residents and tourists. A report by Meituan Dianping, China's largest provider of on-demand online services, said that spending on nighttime dining around the country rose 47 per cent growth of the nighttime catering sector. An unidentified administration official told Xinhua News Agency it would implement identical nighttime and daytime catering service providers. Food safety is the foundation for nighttime catering services, the official said. Only through safe eating can we ensure consumers have a good experience, and the city displays the charm of its late-night cuisine culture.

Fu Yifu, a consumption analyst at Suning Institute of Finance, said the nighttime economy's growth would help boost domestic consumption and create more jobs. Encouraging nighttime business activities will unleash city-dwellers' consumption potential who are busy at work during the daytime. It will also promote the growth of related sectors and spur cities to refine their infrastructure and urban transport.

III

Part Three

*"I have Social Disease. I have to go out every night. If I stay home one night
I start spreading rumours to my dogs."*

-Andy Warhol-

11

Late-night

Andrew Barr's *"Drink: A Social History"* provides another way of thinking about these changing patterns of late-night activity. Barr's account is less about the expansion of work into the night, but more a reminder that our use of time is not ahistorical or universal.[45] As an example, he recounts how breakfast, dinner and the eighteenth-century fashion for lunch occurred at different points in the day for different people. Parisian customs of the nineteenth century, for example, saw different social classes sitting to dine at progressively later times, with the artisan dining at 2 p.m. and *"rich bachelors"* not before 6 p.m.[46] Echoing Amin and Thrift's argument about the ever-changing rhythms of urban life, these examples demonstrate that night and day are not entirely stable concepts.[47] Activities and conduct considered appropriate for one time can just as quickly shift, whether that be due to economic and cultural changes, or the whims of fashion. The late-night city is irrefutably different from the city during the day. There are significant variations around leisure, access, exclusion and economic rationale. Nonetheless, while these current usage patterns may seem thoroughly natural, the *"right"* time to work, eat or socialise is historically and geographically contingent, and likely to change.

According to Jayne's paper considers how geographies of alcohol, drinking and drunkenness have been found within and beyond the discipline of geography.[48] They argue that while there has been a large amount of relevant, detailed and vibrant research considering *"geographical"* issues, alcohol studies have tended to under-theorised the role of space and place. On the other hand, while geographers have been relatively slow to engage with alcohol, drinking and drunkenness, they show that geography has much to offer future research agendas. Despite recent progress, however, a failing of geographers' engagement with alcohol, drinking and drunkenness has been an inability to transcend disciplinary boundaries. They conclude by arguing that geographical research into alcohol, drinking and drunkenness must continue to pursue theoretical and empirical advances and offer policy-relevant *"public geographies"* that speak to non-academic audiences.

Interest of people about late-night activities are different time to time. Google searches for nightclub is higher in 2016.

Searches for: nightclub

Period: 2010-01-01 2022-01-01; Geo: US; Prop: 'web'; Category: all

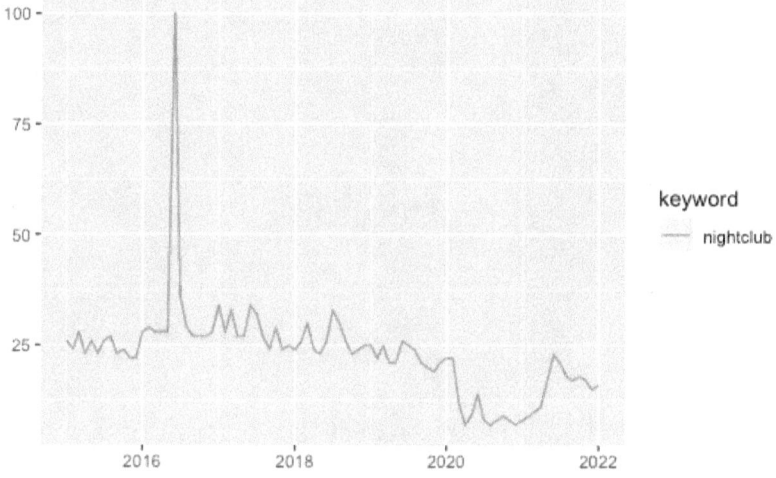

12

Alcohol

Ironically, it was not a European theorist who inspired twenty-four-hour city policies, but a North American. Jane Jacobs' classic work, *"The Death and Life of Great American Cities,"* is well known. Although it had been widely taught to generations of architects and town planners in the UK since its first publication, it somehow failed to reach policy and practice. Jacobs' message was not easy to implement. Basing her ideas on ethnographic observation in New York and Boston, she provided a swingeing critique of comprehensive redevelopment, which she dubbed as *"catastrophic"* and argued instead for incremental change. She was a passionate advocate for dense, mixed-use neighbourhoods, which she demonstrated were not the disorganized slums derided by City Beautiful and Garden City enthusiasts but were the product of *"organized complexity."*

In 2018, the price of alcoholic drinks across the European Union (EU) was more than twice as high in the most expensive Member State than in the cheapest one. When price levels in countries are compared with the EU average price level index of 100, the results show that in 2018, the price of alcoholic drinks (spirits, wine and beer) was highest in Finland (with a price level index of 182), followed by Ireland (177) and Sweden (152).

For people interest...

According to Dick Hobbs, the development of alcohol-based night-time economies as part of government-sponsored post-industrial urban regeneration involves two inter-connected political and economic processes. The first is the shift to a, and the second is the movement within local governance from the provision of services towards a focus upon nurturing economic growth. The violence and disorder that have resulted from the huge expansion in these night-time economies have produced a crisis for state policing that has led, via licensing, to the expansion of commercially relevant control strategies. Hobbs' paper discusses the hypocrisy that is inherent in the governance of liminal licence. Over the past 30 years, British cities have undergone important transformations that should be understood in two closely interconnected political and economic processes. The first is the shift from an economy based upon industrial production to a post-industrial consumer economy. The second is the significant shift in urban governance away from the management of core local services towards a distinct focus upon economic growth. In partnership with the private sector and their own right, local governments have become 'imbued with characteristics once distinctive to businesses – risk-taking, inventiveness, promotion, and profit motivation'. By veering sharply away from Keynesian orthodoxy towards market economics's fluidity as a way of revitalizing economic and private autonomy, the ideological rationale of local government increasingly embraces the free market. This courtship has involved local authorities adopting non-interventionist approaches to economic development. So shifting away from *"municipal socialism,"* whose primary role was to provide local welfare services, towards *"municipal capitalism,"* is increasingly concerned with cultivating local economic growth and development.

The market orientation of regeneration agendas now proceeds largely unchallenged. This clear and unambiguous promotion of the private sector has heralded the city's reinvention as the primary consumption and leisure site. Leisure, in particular, has emerged as a key sector within post-industrial urban economies. Deindustrialization and the decline of the traditional employment base resulted in local government administrators acknowledging that the *"leisure sector"* could play a major part in the twinned processes of urban regeneration and civic renewal. In many British towns and cities, these interrelated developments laid the foundations for creating night-time leisure economies. In an attempt to regenerate and preserve the city centre and promote public usage of increasingly defunct and decrepit public spaces, British towns and cities actively commenced the pursuit of city centre regeneration initiatives. The night-time economy was promoted as central to the image of a modern European city. As *"urban fortunes"* became increasingly bonded to consumption, leisure and tourism, cities began to compete for inward investment.

13

Maps

So, the night-time economy, it's not just about pubs and clubs. According to Boyce's research, the uses of light at night continues to increase. Simply put, this is because, without light, we are deprived of our premier sense, vision. By enabling view, the use of light at night delivers several benefits to people.[49] Such benefits include more excellent safety for pedestrians and drivers, reduced fear of crime, more use of outdoor facilities after dark, enhanced economic growth and the creation of built and natural environments that are a source of beauty and entertainment. This suggests that light at night is linked to some fundamental human motivations, which means that people value such benefits and will not willingly abandon them. Fortunately, careful lighting design, soundly-based outdoor lighting standards and new lighting and sensor technology offer the possibility of providing the benefits of light at night while minimizing the environment's impact.

The night-time economy is increasingly being recognized as a driver of economic growth, but for it to succeed a broad range of professionals need to cultivate it. Whether you work in planning, health, economics, transport, the arts or property – the night-time economy can no longer be an afterthought.

Before moving onto discussing the possibility that assemblage thought and atmosphere might offer for understanding the urban night, it is worth exploring current *"night-time economy studies."* This phrase refers to the mixture of social science studies of alcohol and social science studies of the night-time leisure industry that dominates how we understand night-time cities.

Under an assemblage urbanism approach, this research area can be understood as closing down the assemblages, which make up the night-time city. By making the object of study the *"night-time economy,"* the town at night is reduced, first, to just the bars and clubs which make up city centers, and second, to the *"economic"* ways of relating between these. Even studies within this area that offer a more diverse empirical perspective or have integrated new theoretical approaches into night-time economy studies have not challenged the underlying framework of *"night-time economy"* itself.[50]

The brightest areas of the Earth are the most urbanized, but not necessarily the most populated. Cities tend to grow along coastlines and transportation networks. Even without the underlying map, the outlines of many continents would still be visible. The United States interstate highway system appears as a lattice connecting the brighter dots of city centres. In Russia, the Trans-Siberian railroad is a thin line stretching from Moscow through Asia's centre to Vladivostok. From the Aswan Dam to the Mediterranean Sea, the Nile River is another bright thread through an otherwise dark region.

Even more than 100 years after the electric light invention, some regions remain thinly populated and unlit. Antarctica is entirely dark. The interior jungles of Africa and South America are mostly dark, but lights are beginning to appear. Deserts in Africa, Arabia, Australia, Mongolia, and the United States are poorly lit as well (except along the coast), along with the boreal forests of Canada and Russia, and the magnificent mountains of the Himalaya.

The Earth Observatory article Bright Lights, Big City describes how NASA scientists use city light data (Figures 1,2,3) to map urbanization.[51] Much research has suggested that night-time light (NTL) can be used as a proxy for several variables, including urbanization, density, and economic growth (see chapter 7). Scientists have been using satellite images of Earth at night—often referred to as *"night lights"*—to study human activity and

Figure 1. Earth at Night

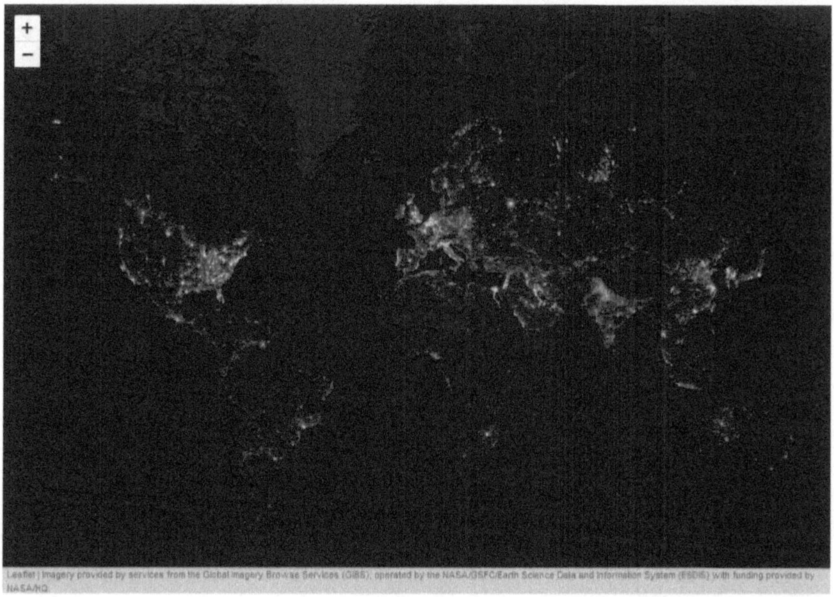

Leaflet | Imagery provided by services from the Global Imagery Browse Services (GIBS), operated by the NASA/GSFC/Earth Science Data and Information System (ESDIS) with funding provided by NASA/HQ.

natural events for almost 30 years. In the past decade, economists have followed suit, realizing that night lights can help gauge economic growth, map poverty, analyze inequality, and tackle numerous questions otherwise impossible to answer, especially in places where data are lacking. In fact, if aliens were ever to approach Earth from its dark side, they would already know some basics about the global economy long before reaching our atmosphere.

Figure 2: EU's nightlights

from the Global Imagery Browse Services (GIBS), operated by the NASA/GSFC/Earth Science Data and Information System (ESDIS) with NASA/HQ funding.

Figure 3: Night Lights of Italy

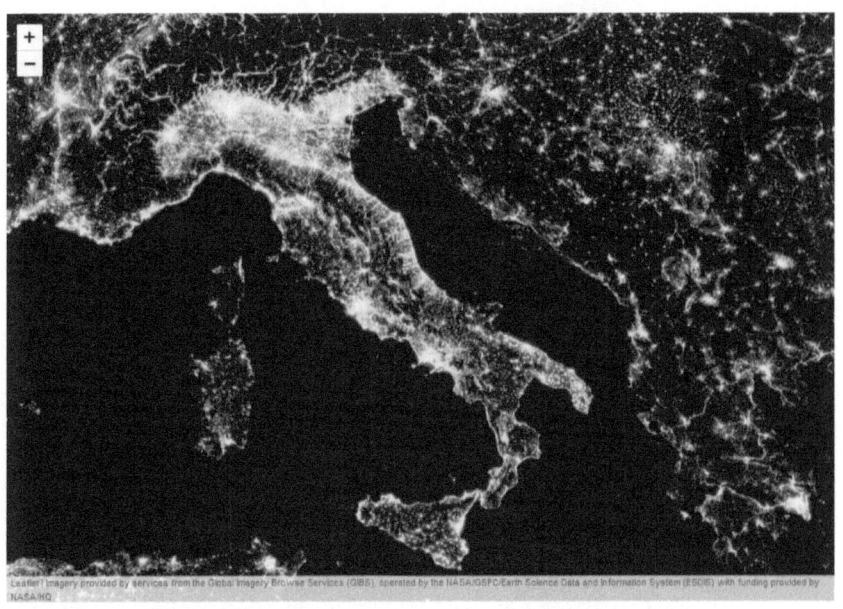

Leaflet | Imagery provided by services from the Global Imagery Browse Services (GIBS), operated by the NASA/GSFC/Earth Science Data and Information System (ESDIS) with funding provided by NASA/HQ.

14

Culture

The night-time economy can have significant impacts on the health and well-being of individuals. Embedding a strategy to promote culture in Local Plans and Town Centre Strategies can also make a difference to an area's night economy's success. These plans, while implemented and written by planners, require political vision and leadership to be successful. The recently released draft London Plan contains, for the first time, a chapter for culture and heritage in addition to City Hall's existing Supplementary Planning Guidance on culture and the night-time economy.

Culture and leisure are vitality essential to peoples' quality of life. A city of Plymouth's size must offer a level of cultural and leisure facilities that meet the needs of its growing population and the sub-regions broader needs. A strong cultural/leisure sector comprises a holistic mix of:

- Individual skills and the opportunity to enhance and develop these,
- A range of accessible, affordable and high-quality culture and leisure facilities where people can develop their skills and interests,
- An active private sector involvement,

- A strong and pro-active voluntary and community (not for profit) sector,
- A public and statutory sector that provides support and resources, where required, for sustainable cultural development.

These are key to creating a thriving, vibrant city and helps create a place where people want to live, work, and visit.

The 1980s saw the gradual recognition of this changing role of culture in the city (and elsewhere). Local government, arts organisations, business people, both companies and umbrella groups such as the Chamber of Commerce, community groups, training organisations and, of course, local artists began to create, often informal coalitions around the elaboration of (formal and informal) cultural strategies aimed at the 'regeneration' of the city centre and the city as a whole. This role of culture in 'regeneration' has been defined in terms of its input into the built environment, the economic benefits of the arts and cultural industries sector, and the re-imaging of the city on the national and international stage. It is right that all these should be included. Still, it is increasingly recognised that, just as a city's deep resources lie within its people's skills and creativity (to which cultural strategies must be central), a city's cultural vibrancy lies in the involvement and identification of the people within its orbit. It is the raised horizons as to what it is possible to do that are important and the decision to do it here.[52]

15

Transport

The paper considers the socio-spatial and temporal dimensions of transport equity for London's NTE in the case study evaluated in McArthur et al.[53]

Their analysis proposes to explore the *"work of framing"* manifested in night-time economy discourses to question how London's nighttime transport strategies attend to issues of socio-spatial disparities and inclusion. Policy frames integrate facts, causal processes and preferences and organize and interpret a complex reality, setting a framework to identify, analyse and respond.[54]

Critically, frames determine what is valid as evidence and how it is interpreted to support decision-making and planning. Our analysis offers new insights about how the transport-economy relationship is framed in policy discourses, assessing whether or not this framing contributes to the design of transport strategies that explicitly account for equity.

The sustainable mobility paradigm has dominated the urban transport research agenda for more than a decade. This paradigm focuses on the environmental impacts of travel and the imperative for climate change mitigation. The specific outcomes of transport in terms of trip type and purpose are not robustly conceptualized, with limited intellectual foundations to understand transport service provision's ethical considerations. McArthur and his colleges' paper critically considers transport strategies recently developed for London's night-time industry, including policy discourse and technical approaches shaping transport services provision at night. Their study evaluates the Spatio-temporal dimensions of equity.

Analysis of policy discourses revealed how nighttime transport is conceived as an instrumental means to grow the night-time industry drawing from the conventional wisdom linking accessibility improvements with economic expansion. This strategy viewed *"London at night"* as a vehicle for economic development, focusing on the economy's consumption side and improving individuals' access to entertainment and recreation. Policy discourse recognised the existence of night-time workers in sectors outside arts and recreation, anyway, attempts to broaden the night-time economy plan to accommodate the travel needs of night-time workers were lost through the limited selection of accessibility metrics used in transport planning practice. This case demonstrates a missed opportunity to improve transport equity across spatial and temporal dimensions.[55] Night-time workers face severe accessibility barriers, often relying on low-frequency bus services with inadequate service coverage across Greater London.

Scrutinising sociospatial and temporal dimensions of transport provision can advance more systematic critical perspectives on transport equity by integrating various distributional issues and linking more closely to the practical barriers faced by nighttime workers to access transport.

IV

Part Four

"I have loved the stars too fondly to be fearful of the night."

-Sarah Williams-

16

Party cities

It is necessary to distinguish between the *"evening"* and the *"late-night"* economies. Initially, this inquiry set out to examine the role of the evening economy in the urban renaissance. Anyway, the evidence which had been received made it clear that in considering the urban renaissance of our city centres, we needed to consider the impact of the late-night economy in addition to the evening economy. There is very little activity in most town and city centres between 5 and 8 o'clock in the evening. Between 5 and 6 o'clock most shops close and people leave work to travel to their homes in the suburbs.

Some, predominantly the young, will then change their clothes and return to the city centres after 8 o'clock to participate in the late-night economy. The late-night economy is centred around the consumption of alcohol. Young people gather in *"vertical drinking"* venues where there are few tables or chairs. They drink standing up, in crowded, bustling environments where music is played at high volume. When these venues close, some will go on to night-clubs which may be open until between 1 and 3 in the morning. Before beginning their journey home, they often buy takeaway food. Older people participating in evening activities tend to go for dinner or to the cinema or theatre.

Very few will drink in city-centre pubs and bars at night.

During the day town and city centres are much more inclusive, offering activities for all age groups. There is no reason why the evening and late-night economies cannot be more inclusive. Evening activity does not have to be focused on alcohol consumption or aimed exclusively at the young. Ideally, people would feel welcome in town and city centres in the evening and late at night. There would be sufficient activity to encourage people to stay after work, instead of going home to the suburbs.

Any major city will have bars, clubs and live music venues, but not all can claim to be a true party capital. And, while the definition of what that is may change from continent to continent, there are a few universal truths. First, a superior party city is fun. The locals like to have a good time, and the nightlife scene is joyous and raucous. Second, there needs to be a diversity of entertainment to cater to all walks of life. Ten clubs spinning the same techno beats is hardly revolutionary. Finally, it should be unique. Whether it's Rio's botecos or Berlin's infamous clubs, every city on this list champions its individuality.

Anyway scoured the globe to find the world's best party cities, from Bangkok to Tel Aviv. And whether you're a dance-'til-sunrise type or prefer whiling away the hours at a hidden bar, there's something for everyone on this travel list. Bangkok, the capital of Thailand, delights every sense, from its beautiful temples to its unforgettable roadside eateries. So it makes sense that the nightlife here is not a one-trick pony. Bangkok's nightlife is so unique because it is diversified.

Visitors can explore and discover new experiences from culture to food, local lifestyle and entertainment. One of the most popular and photogenic areas for nightlife is the Soi Nana district in Chinatown. It's full of converted houses that have been transformed into cozy bars with fun, yet relaxing vibes.

An extra perk: It's easy to grab an order of Chinese dumplings on the street in between bar hops. Bangkok, in general, is known for its robust bar scene. Seven establishments in the city made it onto the coveted list of Asia's 50 Best Bars for 2019, including Thailand's highest ever entry, Bamboo Bar, which ranked No. 8. Those looking for dancing should make a beeline for the Thonglor district in Sukhumvit, where clubs and performing venues offer everything from karaoke to thumping EDM music. In Barcelona, as any student studying abroad can tell you, Barcelona's nightlife stands out for its sheer longevity.

They take partying until dawn quite literally. Of course, in a city where locals don't sit down to dinner until 9 or 10 p.m., it's little wonder that the club scene is still vibrant well into the middle of the night.

The climate along Spain's Mediterranean coast also means that Barcelona's can take advantage of outdoor revelry nearly year-round, so expect plenty of partying on terraces or rooftops. The night scene is mainly divided into two areas. The uptown area includes the famous Aribau and Tuset streets, full of bars and emblematic clubs such as Sutton and Bling Bling. Then, there's the Ciutat Vella district, where popular clubs such as Sala Apolo and Razzmatazz are located. The city is also a hub for music festivals, such as Primavera Sound, Sonar, Tomorrowland and DGTL, which attract artists such as Miley Cyrus and the Killers.

The Beirut waterfront, littered with popular clubs and rooftop bars, maybe the city's most popular party destination, but locals also flock to specific streets, depend- ing on their mood. Gemmayzeh and Mar Mikhael are well-renowned streets that have a traditional feel and are popular for bar-hopping. And Hamra Street has more of a hippie ambience and is popular for its pubs, street cafes and bars.

One activity unites all partiers, however. After a long night out, you can find the party crowd indulging in Lebanese specialities such as manakish (similar to a flatbread) or knife (a sweet cheese pastry), at any number of early-morning breakfast spots. In Berlin, every day is a party.

Whether you're looking to go dancing on a Sunday afternoon or have a big night out on the weekend, you'll have a choice of at least 10 clubs.

The lively vibe of the German capital is still influenced by the events of 1989. During the fall of the Wall, an underground – and illegal – club scene emerged. While most are closed now, the city's spirited party culture remains. The Kreuzberg area is ground zero for exploring the scene. The neighbourhood is special because it is so diverse; you can find a great mix of cultural influences and endless types of restaurants and bars. And of course, all diehard clubbers will want to make a pilgrimage to Berghain, which is famous for its music as for its strict door policy. But if you don't get in, never fear: *"There are no rules; you don't need to dress up, and you can find a party whenever and wherever you like."* Cape Town, with such beautiful surroundings, it's no surprise that Cape Gown partying often happens outdoors. You don't have to be constrained to a bar or club; we have remarkable events, venues and outdoor parties, concierge and front of house manager of The Silo hotel. Popular festivals include Afrika Burn (South Africa's answer to Burning Man) and Rocking the Daisies, which is one of the largest outdoor music festivals in the Southern Hemisphere. Many Capetonians also love to party in the Cape Winelands, where estates and farms surrounding the city host lively events. But a night (or day) out in town is also pretty unique. Capetonians are incredibly laid back, so most venues transform throughout the day from cafes to bars and then to nightclubs. And don't worry about fancy attire: *"There's no stiff formality or dress codes in Cape Town; it's a seaside town at heart."* If there is any city in the world synonymous with partying, it's Las Vegas. But the scene here is more multifaceted than much give it credit for. Few places in the world can boast the high concentration of world-class restaurants, entertainment and nightclubs in such a short distance from one another. The combination of high-quality choices and convenience is a magnet for revellers around the world. While the glittering lights of the Strip offer a party experience for nearly every type of guest, there are a few particularly buzzy spots. The Cosmopolitan, Park MGM, Wynn, and Palms are topping the lists of what's hot right now. Also, Downtown Las Vegas and Chinatown are quickly emerging as must-see destinations. Both neighbourhoods have much more of an edge that is harder to find in the bigger places on the Strip.

As for the veracity of the city's unofficial mantra? *"The Vegas motto – you know the one – unleashes freedom that no other city can claim."* It's got everything, all under a blazing sun and next to the ocean. What also sets Miami apart is how seriously the city takes its nightlife. It's an actual industry here. In Miami, you've got people devoting their lives and careers to making it the best in the world. South Beach still reigns supreme as the city's party capital, with clubs that keep the music going at all hours of the day. LIv, Story, E11even, Rockwell – on any given night you'll see some of the world's biggest athletes, most celebrities or gorgeous models, mixed in with billionaires and anyone else who wants a peek into that lifestyle. But neighbourhoods such as Wynwood (known for its graffiti walls), Downtown and Brickell are also starting to attract crowds. Wherever you go, though, the energy is palpable. It all works in unison: bars, lounges, clubs, hotels, even restaurants throwing parties. It creates this great 24-hour pulsing vibe, which by the way, you can bypass at any moment for an umbrella and beach chair.

From the all-night madness of Times Square's New Year's Eve ball drop to Fashion Week's most exclusive fêtes, New York may be best known for its parties that revolve around its world-famous events. But the City That Never Sleeps also offers a diversity of entertainment for any reveller. New York's variety makes it a world-class party city.

Those looking for a good time in the Big Apple can choose anything from Afro-Latin beats at Bembe in Williamsburg, speakeasies like Employees Only in the West Village, the uninhibited neon circus vibes of the House of Yes in Bushwick, the opulence of the Top of the Standard in the Meatpacking District, to the hard-hitting beats of warehouse-like Good Room in Greenpoint. And, as some of the country's best arbiters of cool, don't expect partiers in this city to follow any rule. Most New Yorkers know that the best parties aren't on the weekends. New Yorkers don't settle for average, and the city is constantly pushing the boundary and exploring new nightlife experiences.

And while every neighbourhood in New York is often pulsing late into the night, people recommend the borough of Brooklyn for those looking for the trendiest spots. It continues to drive the nightlife scene forward: Bushwick, Greenpoint and Williamsburg are where some of the best new parties can be found. One quirk of Rio's nightlife that's a bit unexpected is how early the festivities actually wrap up. In the clubs, the party starts earlier and ends earlier so that you can go to the beach the next day. But the vibrant city certainly makes up for an earlier closing time with its informal botecos, which loosely translates to a bar or watering hole. On weekends, they often play live music, mostly samba and chorinho, and people dance on the street to the tunes. The hottest neighbourhoods for partying are Lapa, Centro and Botafoga, but one club reigns supreme:

One of the largest clubs in South America has two dance floors, aerialists, and, unusual for the city, stays open until 7 a.m. Sunday. But when in doubt, dip into any bar: *"Very rarely will you see an empty club or bar on a Friday or Saturday night,"* says Jon Hillstead, a senior travel consultant with South America. Most young Cariocas are people who are huge into the nightlife scene. They love music, dancing, drinking and overall, just being social.

A common refrain about the South Korean people is that they work hard and play hard. Nowhere is this dichotomy more evident than in Seoul. Everyone from students to business people is known for logging impossibly long hours, followed by partying with wild abandon once their duties (or homework) are complete. In the city's multi-level clubs, it's not uncommon for them to be crowded until well after the sun rises, with revellers then decamping immediately for the nearest Korean barbecue restaurant. Students and younger folk flock to the Hongdae area, which is known for its underground music scene. Those looking for a high-end party go to Gangnam, which is a combination of West Coast plus New York City-style in one area.

Many may be familiar with the area because of Psy's song *"Gangnam Style"* from 2012, but it's famous in its own right for venues such as Octagon and Arena. One of Tel Aviv's informal mottos is *"the city that never stops"*, and its club scene is certainly indicative of that. Compared to cities in Europe and the United States, in Tel Aviv, you go out pretty late at night. Many clubs open their doors around midnight or later and sometimes stay open until 6 o'clock in the morning. A bonus is the (lack of a) dress code: The scene is easy going and nonformal, which means much more fun. Serious partiers know to hit up Rothschild Boulevard come nightfall. It's the place to see and be seen. It features trendy bars, clubs and cafes, and it's alive and kicking 24/7. Another popular neighbourhood is Florentin, which Borochoff says is similar to Chelsea in New York City or Shoreditch in London. Many hipsters, artists and bohemian people live there. Wherever you visit, there is a sense of the global melting pot. In Israel, people from more than 100 nationalities come together. This multicultural atmosphere is apparent throughout the parties thrown all across town.

17

The city that never sleeps

John Rechy's inaugural novel *The City of Night* (1963) is strategi-
cally situated in New York City. As the narrator says in the quote
"The world of Times Square was a world which I was certain I had sought out willingly – not a world which had sum-
moned me. And because I believe that, its lure, for me,
  was much more powerful."
There are plenty of late-night options in the city that never sleeps.
For a unique drinking experience, visit Pouring Ribbons—the bar rates
each cocktail on two scales: refreshing to spirituous, and comforting
to adventurous. Guests can choose their adventure, and also sample
from the bar's extensive charcuterie menu. Dead Rabbit provides a
more informal drinking atmosphere. The bar's ground floor taproom
offers craft beer, bottled punch, and whiskies, while the upstairs
parlour features 72 cocktails based on different historical periods. The
Experimental Cocktail Club on the city's Lower East Side also offers
innovative cocktails in a low-lit, vintage setting.
According to Dan Q. Dao's article *"The Absolute Best Nightclubs And
Lounges In New York City"* While social media and dating apps have
perhaps reduced the perceived need for in-person socializing and

meeting new people, platforms like Instagram have also allowed us to discover new venues and parties in real-time. That, in turn, has pushed proprietors and party masters to create new attention-worthy experiences and moments that'll inspire people to get off their couches. And it's in part thanks to the technology of ride services like Lyft and Uber that there's now plenty of cool to be found above and beyond 14th Street in Manhattan.[56]

It is one of the best places on earth to be truly alive when the sun goes down. In New York, there are plenty of places to go... NYC is rightfully known for its nightlife. Whether that means sophisticated cocktail dens, friendly dive bars or bottle-service-only dance clubs, the City's after-dark entertainment is just as electrifying as it ever was. You may have heard that New York City nightlife is dead, but don't be fooled—the party goes on. In fact, according to the first-ever economic impact study of local nightlife by the New York Mayor's Office of Media and Entertainment, nightlife in the city is growing faster than the rest of the overall economy, with jobs and wages up by annual rates of 5 and 8 per cent, respectively.

Positively, much of this has to do with the expanding definition of nightlife: it's not just DJ-driven clubs, but also late-night restaurants, pubs and cocktail bars, and after-hours sports and recreation. But there's also something to be told for how diverse, both in style and geography, the NYC nightlife experience has become.

Whether you're looking to trick with sparklers and courage service or dance the night away in an underground warehouse, you'll surely find what you're after once the sun goes down.

* * *

London is not only the capital of England but also the most populous city in the UK. London's nightlife offers something for everyone—from comedy cabarets to swanky boutique bars, you don't have to look far for late-night entertainment. Dusty blue walls and romantic decor make the Blue Bar a favourite upscale cocktail spot. Located in the Berkeley Hotel, it offers live jazz music and an inventive cocktail menu. For a more traditional pub experience, try Jerusalem Tavern. The pub's small interior belies an extensive list of St. Peter's beers and ale, and the laid-back atmosphere creates a pleasant drinking experience. For arts and culture aficionados, the Royal Opera House is a must. The venue hosts nightly performances, including classical ballets and opera.

British people like going to pubs where they can have a snack and drink a pint of beer. The incidence of drunkenness in town centres is not new. Ackroyd describes how London has been awash with alcohol at various times in its long history.[57] Each market town delights in the numbers of historic pubs it contains. Although the twentieth century is normally portrayed as one in which the strict licensing laws introduced during the First World War led to sobriety, the 1980s saw a concern with *"lager louts"*[58] in provincial towns and champagne excesses by *"hooray Henrys"*[59] in the cities.[60] The optimistic quotation from Worpole in the early 1990s came from his analysis of the trends which he and his associates thought would lead towards more inclusive, less alcohol-based night-time activities in towns and cities.

18

Back to the island

Locating Ibiza on the map may be more or less comfortable, depending on where you're from and your geography knowledge. Ibiza (Catalan: *Eivissa*) is a Spanish island in the Mediterranean Sea off Spain's eastern coast.

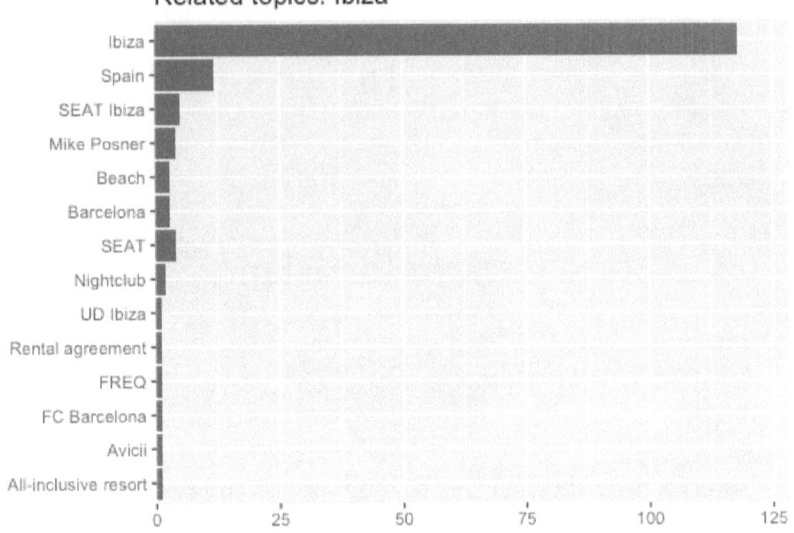

Related topics: Ibiza

Ibiza has become well known for its association with nightlife, elec-
tronic dance music, and the summer club scene, all of which attract
many tourists drawn to that holiday type. Several years before 2010, the
island's government and the Spanish Tourist Office had been working
to promote more family-oriented tourism. The police closed down
clubs that played music at late night hours, but by 2010 this policy was
reversed. Around 2015 it was resumed.

Ibiza is administratively part of the Balearic Islands' autonomous
community, whose capital is Palma, on the island of Majorca. Ibiza
comprises 5 of the community's 67 municipalities.

The Old Town (Dalt Vila) is an ancient sandstone fortress, built as a
defence against pirates and other invaders. It's one of the best things
to do in Ibiza, and walking through the ancient gate into the city is
evocative. The town itself has retained a timeless feel.

You'll find some exciting shopping, along with some generations-old
bodegas for a refreshing drink and bite to eat. From the top of the hill,

you get some great views down to the marina and the newer districts of Ibiza Town.

Ibiza is one of the most famous places in the world for nightlife. It's full of superclubs, party hotels, beach bars and some really, really nice restaurants. During the summer months, many of the world's leading DJs take up residences in the superclubs and hotels. And if you fancy joining them, here's our guide to the island's best nightlife - as well as a few suggestions for when you need a night off.

During the summer months, Ibiza's all about the superclubs, which are largely found outside of town. They can be expensive (it's best to go for drinks at a bar in town first), they really are where the party's at, and should be experienced at least once.

Pacha has been open since 1973. It's just outside Ibiza Town and is the only superclub that opens year-round. Specialising in House music, residencies during the summer months include the world's biggest DJs, like David Guetta. For something a bit different, try the smaller downstairs spaces - the Global and Funky Rooms. That's where you'll find a more diverse musical line-up, including R&B, hip-hop and disco, and occasionally stage live gigs. You can also chill out under the stars on Pacha's rooftop terrace and restaurant.

Officially the world's biggest nightclub, Privilege is big enough to host up to 10,000 clubbers. It's a vast aircraft hangar-like space, found just outside the village of San Rafael. Underneath its 25 metres high ceiling you'll find gardens, chill-out areas, an impressive dome and lavish stage sets.

Amnesia is now over 40 years old, one of the island's most beloved clubbing institutions. It's never far from the world's best club lists. Found between Ibiza Town and San Rafael, it's famous for its superstar DJs - including Carl Cox and Paul Van Dyk. It's regular, and well-known parties include Cream, Music On and Cocoon. But the real star is its technical specs. The club's custom-made sound system is one of the most powerful around. The dance floor is surrounded by ice cannons, which blast revellers with a plume of cooling, and very cool-looking, fog. The stage is equally impressive, DJs perform from within a giant high-tech pyramid set.

Formerly known as Space, Hï is by Playa d'en Bossa beach, west of Ibiza town. It's got awe-inspiring light shows and an equally impressive view from the open-air terraces. There's even a DJ booth in the club's unisex bathroom. One of Hï's biggest parties is Glitterbox, who host two nights of classic disco and house music a week. Expect some of the island's most glamorous dancers and a wild 'anything goes' attitude.

Based in San Antonio town centre, Eden is probably the most accessible of Ibiza's superclubs. Previously home to Gatecrasher and Pete Tong, it's now a massive theatre-like space after a major facelift. Besides regular club nights from house and trance names like Defected, Eden will be hosting more gigs and live music events.

DC10 is an alternative to the more slick superclubs. Found in a former Finca right by the airport, DC10 is a little more off the beaten track. What it lacks in glitz and glamour, it more than makes up for in tunes. Specialising in techno, and with parties that regularly spill out onto the open-air terrace, DC10 is a club for those who take their music seriously.

San Antonio's beachfront bars are famous for their views. Not just of the shimmering waters of the Mediterranean, but the uninterrupted sunset. Sitting back with a drink at Cafe Mambo or Cafe del Mar and watching the sun go down is an Ibiza tradition. The sight is often so spectacular that it draws applause from the strip's patrons.

One of the most exclusive spots to spend the day on the island, Nikki Beach is a beach club, restaurant, pool, bar and boutique, just outside of Santa Eulalia. At weekends during the summer, the club stays open until late. Head there for a very nice open-air dinner.

Ibiza's original hippy spirit is alive on the north coast. Every Sunday evening during the summer, thousands gather on the beach to "drum down the sunset". It's become one of the most popular parties around, and so it can be difficult to find somewhere to park if you turn up too late in the day. But despite the crowds, the laid-back vibe remains. Head down early on in the day to bag a spot - there's a nearby colourful flea market nearby, or beach-front bars and restaurants while you're waiting.

During the summer, Ibiza is almost as popular with sailing enthusiasts as it is with clubbers. And you'll find plenty of boat parties setting off from the island's harbours. The biggest, and possibly the best, is Pukka Up, which sets sail from San Antonio twice a week. Tickets to Pukka Up's boat parties will normally also include entry to one of the island's superclubs after you get back to shore, so make for a good value night.

19

The party never ends

The party never ends! The party never ends in Berlin, as late-night venues are open until the early hours of the morning.

The Victoria Bar's intimate, *70s* style lounge is the perfect place to enjoy a drink. The bar's artsy decor and well-dressed bartenders will take you back to a different era, and old-school cocktails are the epitome of stylish elegance. Green Door, another one of the city's retro lounges, features expertly crafted drinks and quirky decor—the walls are covered with gingham wallpaper, and stand-alone lamps line the bar.

Berlin is the capital and largest city of Germany by both area and population. It is 3,748,148 (2018) inhabitants make it the second-most populous city proper of the European Union after London.

The city is one of Germany's 16 federal states. The state of Brandenburg surrounds it, and contiguous with Potsdam, Brandenburg's capital. The two cities are at the centre of the Berlin-Brandenburg capital region, with about six million inhabitants and more than 30,000 km², Germany's third-largest metropolitan region after the Rhine-Ruhr and Rhine-Main regions.

Berlin straddles the River Spree banks, which flows into the River Havel (a tributary of the River Elbe) in the western borough of Spandau.

Among the city's main topographical features are the many lakes in the west and southeastern districts formed by the Spree, Havel, and Dahme rivers (Lake Muggelsee). Due to its location in the European Plain, Berlin is influenced by a temperate seasonal climate. About one-third of the city's area comprises forests, parks, gardens, rivers, canals and lakes. The city lies in the Central German dialect area, the Berlin dialect being a variant of the Lusatian-New Marchian dialects.

First documented in the 13th century and situated at the crossing of two important historic trade routes, Berlin became the capital of the Margraviate of Branden- burg (1417–1701), the Kingdom of Prussia (1701–1918), the German Empire (1871–1918), the Weimar Republic (1919–1933), and the Third Reich (1933–1945). Berlin in the 1920s was the third-largest municipality in the world.

After World War II and its subsequent occupation by the victorious countries, the city was divided; West Berlin became a de facto West German exclave, surrounded by the Berlin Wall (1961–1989) and East German territory. East Berlin was declared the capital of East Germany, while Bonn became the West German capital. Following German reunification in 1990, Berlin once again became the capital of all of Germany.

Berlin is a world city of culture, politics, media and science. Its economy is based on high-tech firms and the service sector, encompassing a diverse range of creative industries, research facilities, media corporations and convention venues. Berlin serves as a continental hub for air and rail traffic and has a highly complex public transportation network. The metropolis is a popular tourist destination. Significant industries also include IT, pharmaceuticals, biomedical engineering, clean tech, biotechnology, construction and electronics.

Berlin is home to world-renowned universities such as the Humboldt Universitat Zu Berlin (HU Berlin), the Technische Universitat Berlin (TU Berlin), the Freie Uni- Universitat Berlin (Free University of Berlin), the Universitat der Kunste (University of the Arts) and the Berlin School of Economics and Law. The city has numerous orchestras, museums, and entertainment venues, and is host to many sporting events. Its Zoological Garden is the most visited zoo in Europe and one of the most popular worldwide. With the world's oldest large-scale movie studio complex, Berlin is an increasingly popular location for international film productions. The city is well known for its festivals, diverse architecture, nightlife, contemporary arts, and very high quality of living since the 2000s Berlin has seen the emergence of a cosmopolitan entrepreneurial scene.

In Germany, google searching...

20

Most fashionable city

Today you look good! It does not compliment for Milan, because Milan is always beautiful. The style looks different all over the world, although some cities are known for being particularly fashionable. For example, residents of London, England, have a reputation for setting street style trends, while New York City sets the tone by being home to several fashion schools. A fashion capital is a city that has a significant influence on international fashion trends. The design, production and retailing of fashion products, plus events such as fashion weeks, awards and trade fairs all generate significant economic output.

Milan is not only the golden location of the fashion and design industries as well as high-tech research centres. The cities considered the global *"Big Four"* fashion capitals of the 21st century are Milan, London, New York and Paris.

Usually, Milan was ranked as the most stylish city in the world. Italy is full of smart cities, and Milan is one of them. The city's fashion week is world-renowned, making Milan appealing to designers, stylists, and modelling agencies. The city is home to classic fashion houses like Armani, Dolce Gabbana, Versace, and Italian versions of magazines like *"Vogue"* and *"Vanity Fair."* Milan is a city in northern Italy, capital of Lombardy, and the second-most populous city in Italy after Rome, with the city proper having a population of 1,395,274. In contrast, its metropolitan city has a population of 3,259,835. Unadulterated sophistication defines Milan, a city with a rich history and fashion heritage. Milanese fashion is most known for quality textiles and fabrics.

Milan's fashion industry's peculiar nature is to reunite what capitalism normally divides: *conception and execution, big and small, design and production.*

The ecosystem of the fashion industry is composed of giants (stylists like Armani and Valentino, Prada and Dolce e Gabbana, Marras, Gucci and so on) and a myriad of artisans, art masters, modellers and tailors able to capture the always changing and contradictory demands of the fashion world.

According to M. D'Ovidio's *"Moda e manifattura a Milano, in Milano Produttiva"* (Milan Chamber of Commerce), the conception of fashion products by creative people is a diffused practice, made by a community of different players. The dimension of such a phenomenon is very impressive. The direct employment is made up of 37.500 employees distributed through 6.000 enterprises (the average dimension of the typical unit of production being 6 employees), but 1/5 of the total value added of the Milanese economy is directly or indirectly connected the fashion industry.[61]

So, fashion enterprises' local constellation creates a wider district including Milan, Busto Arsizio, Como, Varese, Monza, Vigevano specialized in different products and production chains (from silk to shoes, from textile to fashion design). The miracle is that, notwithstanding the overall globalization and delocalization trends, the different phases of conception, design and production are still reunited here: making the daily exchange of knowledge and the quick adjustments to demand variations still possible. However, the production is made in a range of

60 kilometres from Milan.

V

Part Five

"Cities, like cats, will reveal themselves at night."

-Rupert Brooke-

21

Back to the features

Hobbs focuses upon the emergence of the night-time economy both materially and culturally as a powerful manifestation of post-industrial society.[62] This emergence features two fundamental processes: firstly a shift in economic development from the industrial to the post-industrial; secondly a significant orientation of urban governance involving a move away from the traditional managerial functions of local service provision, towards an entrepreneurial stance primarily focused on the facilitation of economic growth. Central to this new industrial era is the identification and promotion of liminality.

The State's apparent inability to control these new leisure zones constitutes creating an urban frontier governed by commercial imperatives.

The key to a better night in the city is shifting mindsets about the night and becoming proactively involved in planning for the city's social, cultural, and economic activities between 6 pm and 6 am. A city's night-time signals whether or not a place is safe, affordable, equitable and innovative. Night-time businesses need City services just as much as any other business. By investing in the night-time economy, it can strengthen the city's daytime economy and overall livability. Planning an economy at night is a new role for cities. It is so unique that there is no standard mechanism for tracking the number of businesses that operate at night or how many people work at night. There are several reasons why local development has traditionally overlooked night-time. On a functional level, many people who are employed by regional government offices and in other traditional office settings, work during the day from 9 am to 5 pm. The daytime economy is already a challenging and complex portfolio for any local government.

Night-time may be used for networking with business clients through events, conferences or meetings. Still, rarely is it approached with the expertise, resources or consideration that daytime is given. The impact of residential living growth in the downtown core has a push and pull factor for the city's night-time economy. As the size of condominiums in the downtown are mostly small, non-residential leisure spaces are valued neighborhood amenities. Stakeholders mentioned that the restaurants, bars, outdoor patios, games rooms and live music venues in the downtown core are the residents' kitchens, living rooms and backyards. On the other hand, the growth of residential development in the downtown core has meant an increase in property prices overall and puts pressure on leisure activities in the downtown core to wrap-up or shut down by 11 pm. Improved planning of the city at night will help residents who live near or beside vibrant night-time scenes.

22

Regulation

The interest to regulate night-time behaviour is not new. Government policy is paradoxically torn between a vibrant night-time economy's economic benefits, open all hours, and the regulatory concerns of noise, nuisance, incivilities, and violence. So, the night-time economy is increasingly being recognized as a driver of economic growth, but for it to succeed a broad range of professionals need to cultivate it. Whether you work in planning, health, economics, transport, the arts or property – the night-time economy can no longer be an afterthought.

Cities can increase their productivity by adopting measures that regulate and diversify the array of social and economic activities that take place during the night. In the 1990s, some UK cities stopped seeing the night as negative and problematic space and began to estimate the value of the so-called *"night-time economy:"* the contributions made to city coffers by restaurants, nightclubs, taxis and other night-time services and forms of entertainment. Some cities have made good progress in promoting their night-time economies.

For instance, in 2007 the City of London published a document titled *Managing the Night-Time Economy*, a guide to nocturnal best practices that describes the regulatory framework and the primary interventions that have made the British capital a night-time city model for both residents and visitors. From London's practice and that of other cities around the world, it can be identified at least five reasons why cities should promote their night-time economies.

The night-time economy is a source of employment and additional revenue for local governments. According to TBR's Night-Mix Index, the UK's night-time economy employs 1.3 million people and is worth £66bn a year.[63] This index analyses the composition of the night-time economy in different areas of the city by measuring indicators such as the number, type and size of the businesses; the number of people that work during this time frame, the evolution of the area's night-time economy, and its growth in comparison to other sectors of the local economy.

It allows local administrations to diversify their leisure and commercial activities. The night-time economy is an opportunity to revitalize urban areas that become deserted at night. For instance, by organising food festivals and restaurants and bars in the city centre, cities like London can retain more people in these commercial areas, reducing the number of commuters that return home right after work. This not only results in greater revenue for these businesses but also, helps alleviate rush-hour congestion.

It promotes greater citizen security. By prolonging stores' and restaurants' hours of operation, cities can keep their streets lively and safe. A few years ago, the night in Brixton (a district of South London) was seen as a synonym of crime and violence. The majority of the bars closed at the same time, leaving hundreds of drunken youngsters in the street. To solve this problem, the city licensed new bars, clubs and pop-up restaurants in the area, to diversify the area's night-time activities.

It boosts local tourism. The most attractive tourist destinations are those that offer an array of entertainment options for different ages, cultures and lifestyles, including families. This requires private as well as public attractions and night-time leisure activities not associated with the consumption of alcohol. Somerset House is a fashionable multi-use open space in London. Part government and part academic building, this neoclassical structure is also a concert hall, fashion venue and art gallery. During winter nights, its ice rink becomes a dance floor where some of Europe's best DJs play their music for visitors of all ages.

Creates a greater sense of belonging. A city that offers a wide variety of activities, good lighting, security and public transportation, invites its citizens to explore it during the day as well as during the night. In this sense, a healthy night-time economy can help build a neighborhood's identity and create a strong sense of belonging for those who live in it.

For all these reasons, it is essential to boost our municipalities' night-time economies. Anyway, we must consider that elements such as qualified local police and improved street lighting are crucial to creating 24-hour cities.

In that sense, London has a competitive advantage. Also, local governments must work side by side with all actors—neighborhood associations, bar owners, taxi companies, local police, sanitation and health services—to identify what are the best ways to regulate noise and improve garbage collection, among other issues, without hurting the businesses in the area. In Latin America, cities like Asuncion (Paraguay) are working in this direction. The municipality, the National Culture Office and the National Tourism Office, organised meetings to discuss night-time activities in the historical centre to commemorate the city anniversary. These entities created a multi-sectoral team—government, neighbors and businesses—to monitor the festivities and ensure their positive economic impact on the city.

23

Municipal policy

For municipal politicians and urban entrepreneurs alike, the stress upon market ideology created a fog of *city boosterism*[64] shrouding the heavy episodic alcohol consumption that lay at the heart of the night-time economy.[65] The new urban script, which promised a *"cafe society,"* for the most part, delivered only a flow of capital into the development of venues selling alcohol. In economic terms, alcohol is the core commodity that attracts individuals into the night-time city.[66] Moreover, alcohol-based culture nourishes many complementary markets, such as fast food outlets and taxi services.

In cultural terms, alcohol bestows a legal methodology for altering the mundane, pressurised, regimented and unattractive world of daylight comportment, realigning meaning and understanding to fit a more seductive and alluring world of hedonism and carnival.[67]

The mass development of licensed premises tends rapidly to inundate an area, because the alcohol industry, seeking to reduce commercial risks, commonly invests in locations where the formula for profit is already well established. Jacobs' ensuing clustering of alcohol outlets has as alluded to over 60 years ago, clear implications for crime and disorder.[68]

Scholars have offered several explanations for the increasing importance of civic entrepreneurship. These include the demands of market forces created in the context of globalization and the consequent loss of local economic sovereignty, the demise of *"Keynesian interventionism"*[69] and the hegemony of *"enterprise culture."* [70]

In the new economic context, all places are *"forced to play the same game,"* yet not all locations can be equally successful, for there will always be both 'losers' and 'winners'. Proactive strategies designed to secure a competitive advantage over perceived rivals' have usually involved *"re-imaging"* and *"place-marketing"* initiatives designed to attract investment from external and 'mobile' capital, to attract an influx of skilled and professional residents, and to boost the local tourism, leisure and retail sectors.[71]

This urban *"beauty contests"* often centre around *"flagship"* projects such as waterfront developments, heritage and theme parks, concert halls, shopping centers, prestigious office and leisure complexes, and the hosting of significant cultural and sporting events.[72]

Although the night-time economy's growth must be situated within these transformative processes, a range of other factors has aided its emergence as a critical post-industrial economic and cultural arena. The night-time economy's support structures have included such diverse inducements as innovative parking developments, traffic and public transport regimes, city centre street lighting, door supervisor registration schemes, and high-profile civil policing patrols.

A liberal approach to alcohol and entertainment licensing and planning applications can act as a powerful lure to nomadic capital on the administering head. Direct financial inducements in the form of grants and loans may also be made available to encourage investment from brewers, entrepreneurs and leisure corporations. The obvious placements in the night-time economy constitute anew focus for post-industrial economic power. The existence of a thriving night-time economy is now taken as a precondition for any urban centre wishing to make a statement concerning its progressive status.[73]

Local politicians now proclaim a phoenix-like rise from the ashes for ex-industrial cities; this transforms not only bricks and mortar but also traditional systems of bourgeois control over urban leisure, which also had their foundations deep in the Victorian era. This shift in economic and social life's rhythm stands in stark but lucrative contrast to our traditional perception of the night.

This contrast corresponds to a conflict that is integral to our under-standing of the essential ambiguity of nightlife. Yet, by the dawn of a new millennium town, planners and city managers were beginning to admit to the hard reality beneath the glossy rhetoric of the 24-hour city: that the night-time economy is as dependent upon hedonistic drives cultivated in the alcohol youth nexus as industrial society was on the motive power of coal and steam.[74] As Osborne and Rose remark, *"urban govern-mentality uses the insidious ungovernability of the city as a resource and an inspiration."* There is no denying the *"multiplication of urban spaces"* that typifies late modernity, or the market differentiation that is a feature of some of the more developed night-time economies.[75] That a complex and mixed economy may be the planning professional's ideal.[76] Empirically, however, it is impossible to resist the conclusion that – in Britain at least – it is youth that dominates a night-time economy that constitutes an imperfectly regulated zone of quasi-liminality awash on a sea of alcohol.

24

Good night

A global view on urban night-time policy and governance shows various approaches across Europe, Asia, North and South America. Until recently, management of the city at night has been dominated by developing and growing night-time economies around entertainment, leisure and consumption. This is focused on central business districts, historic areas linked to tourism, and new development zones planned and designed for night-specific uses. In recent years, discussions of the city at night have broadened to incorporate the needs of residents, workers and linked infrastructure. However, along with rapid urbanization, night-time activities from places, such as restaurants, pubs and bars, and theatres, have created enormous economic and social benefits. As a newly developed social phenomenon, the night-time economy has been used to describe economic activities at night.

The significant findings from the literature review are that the night-time economy is not new and not unique. The night-time economy in cities is often overlooked because night-time activities are not visible during the day and not widely recognized as a valued contributor to the economy. The academic research also points to potential benefits of creating night-time strategies. For example, the night-time economy can be a new way of addressing creative city development, developing a more robust twenty-four-hour economy by supporting local businesses, linking daytime and night-times through *"cross-over"* activities spaces, increasing safety, and detecting upcoming day time trends.

Certainly, however, the most important aspect of the presence of night-time activities are refreshment. Being able to have a good night's sleep is essential for individual health. People who work often spend more time in their homes asleep than awake. A resident must be able to have the time to rest and be quiet when they choose to. A good night's sleep can be achieved, without threatening night-time businesses, when cities actively plan for night-time use.

I don't know why people searching *"good night"* in google, however the graph below shows related quires.

Good Night!

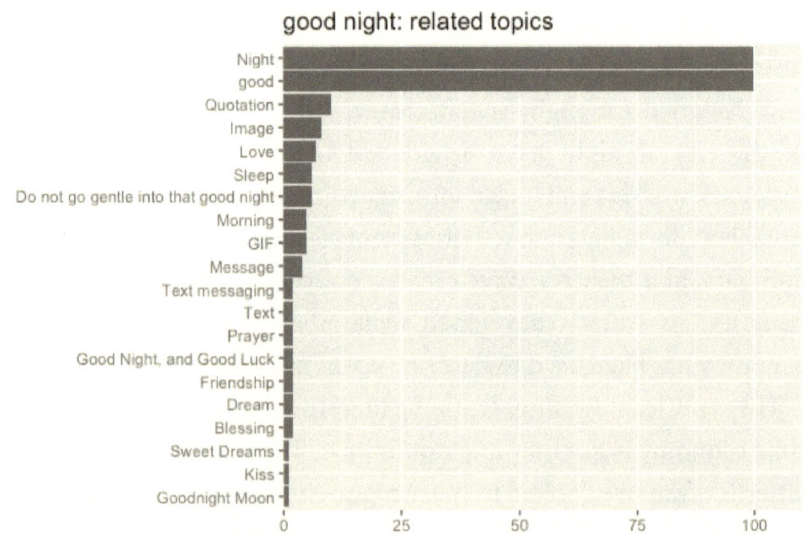

For comments and suggestions write to @avetisyansergeyauthur on Facebook & Instagram, and @SergejAvetisyan on Twitter. All the suggestions and comments are appreciated and will be included in the updated version of the book.

Notes

BACKSTORY VIBES

1   I am joking it is not at 11:11 pm. Actually, I do not remember; it was several years ago.

2   Eco, U. (1984), *The role of the reader: Explorations in the semiotics of texts*, volume 318. Indiana University Press.

3   Soja, E. (2003), *Writing the city spatially*. City, 7(3):269–280.

4   Florida, R. (2014), *The rise of the creative class–revisited: Revised and expanded*. Basic Books (AZ).

NIGHTLIFE

5   See Hannigan, (2005), *Fantasy City: Pleasure and Profit in the postmodern metropolis*, Routledge.

6   Lovatt and O'Connor, (1995), *Cities and the night-time economy*. Planning Practice Research, 10(2): 127–134.

7   Rowe, D. (2007), *Midnight ramblers are spoiling city life*. Sydney Morning Herald, 19.

ORIGINS OF TERM

8   *The Great Good Place* is a book by Ray Oldenburg, originally published in 1989. More recent reprints have occurred in 1997 and 1999. While *"Cafes, Coffee Shops, Community Centers, General Stores, Bars, Hangouts, and How They Get You through the Day"* was the original subtitle, the renaissance of this work uses the new sub- title *"Cafes, Coffee Shops, Bookstores, Bars, Hair Salons and Other Hangouts at the Heart of a Community."*

9   Bianchini, F. (1995), *Night cultures, night economies*. Planning Practice Research, 10(2):121–126.

10   Mulgan, G., Worpole, K., et al.(1986), *Saturday night or Sunday morning? From arts to industry-new forms of cultural policy*. Comedia Publishing Group.

11   Montgomery, J. (1990), *Cities and the art of cultural planning*. Planning Practice and Research,5(3):17–24.

12   Bianchini, F. (1995), *Night cultures, night economies.* Planning Practice Research, 10(2):121–126; Out of hours: a study of economic, social and cultural life in twelve town cen-tres in the uk-summary report.Out of hours: a study of economic, social and cultural life in twelve town centresin the UK-summary report.; Heath, T. (1997), *The twenty-four-hour city concept—a review of initiatives in British cities.* Journal of Urban Design, 2(2):193–204.

13   Bianchini, F. (1995), *Night cultures, night economies.* Planning Practice & Research, 10(2):121–126.

ASSEMBLAGE

14   Bianchini, (1995), *Night cultures, night economies.* Planning Practice Research, 10(2):121–126.

15   Heath, T. (1997), *The twenty-four-hour city concept—a review of initiatives in British cities.* Journal of Urban Design, 2(2):193–204.

PLANNING'S ROLE

16   James Wilson Rouse (April 26, 1914 – April 9, 1996) was an American businessman and founder of The Rouse Company. Rouse was a pioneering American real estate developer, urban planner, civic activist, and later, free enterprise-based philanthropist. He received the Presidental Medal of Freedom, the highest civilian award, for his lifetime achievements.

17   See book, Woodward, I., Taylor, J., & Bennett, A. (Eds.). (2014). *The Festivalization of Culture.* Ashgate Publishing, Ltd.. According to Woodward, Taylor, and Bennett, *"The Festivalisation of Culture explores the links between various local and global cultures, communities, identities and lifestyle narratives as they are both constructed and experienced in the festival context. Drawing on a wide range of case studies from Australia and Europe, festivals are examined as sites for the performance and critique of lifestyle, identity & cultural politics; as vehicles for the mobilization and cementation of local and global communities; and as spatio-temporal events that inspire and determine meaning in peoples' lives. Investigating the manner in which festivals are no longer merely periodic, cultural, religious or historical events within communities, but rather a popular means through which citizens consume and experience culture, this book also sheds light on the increasing diversity of contemporary societies and the role played by festivals as sites of cohesion, cultural critique and social mobility. As such, this book will be of interest to those working in areas such as the sociology, consumption and commodification of culture, social and cultural geography, anthropology, cultural studies and popular music studies."*

18   Somers, D. (1971), *The leisure revolution: recreation in the American City, 1820–1920,* Journal of Popular Culture 5 (Summer): 125–47.

19   Helms, G. (2012), *Towards safe city centres?: Remaking the spaces of an Old-Industrial City*, Ashgate Publishing, Ltd.; Van Liempt, I., (2014), Safe nightlife collaborations: multiple actors, conflicting interests and different power distributions. Urban Stud. http://dx.doi.org/ 10.1177/0042098013504010.

DEINDUSTRIALIZATION

20   Harvey, D. (1989). *The urban experience*. JHU Press.

21   Zukin, S. (1989). *Loft living: Culture and capital in urban change*. Rutgers University; Press.; Lloyd, R. (2010). Neo-bohemia: Art and commerce in the postindustrial city. Routledge.; Bourdieu, P. et al. (1984), *A social critique of the judgement of taste*. Traducido del francespor R. Nice. Londres, Routledge.

22   Hall, (1988), *The city of theory. The city reader*, pages 391–393.

ECONOMICS

23   Henderson, J. V., Storeygard, A., and Weil, D. N. (2012). *Measuring economic growth fromouter space*. American economic review, 102(2):994–1028.

24   A neural network is a network or circuit of neurons, or in a modern sense, an artificial neural network, composed of artificial neurons or nodes. Thus, a neural network is either a biological neural network, made up of real biological neurons or an artificial neural network, for solving artificial intelligence problems. The connections of the biological neuron are modelled as weights. A positive weight reflects an excitatory connection, while negative values mean inhibitory connections. All inputs are modified by weight and summed. This activity is referred to as a linear combination. Finally, an activation function controls the amplitude of the output.

25   Chen, X. and Nordhaus, W. D. (2010), *The value of luminosity data as a proxy for economic statistics*, Technical report, National Bureau of Economic Research.

26   Mellander, C., Lobo, J., Stolarick, K., and Matheson, Z. (2015). Night-time light data: A good proxy measure for economic activity? PloS one, 10(10):e0139779.

27   Doll, C. N., Muller, J.-P., and Morley, J. G. (2006). Mapping regional economic activity from night-time light satellite imagery. Ecological Economics, 57(1):75–92.

28   Bundervoet et al., (2015), Bright lights, big cities: measuring national and subnational economic growth in Africa from outer space, with an application to Kenya and Rwanda. The World Bank

29   Forbes, D. J. (2005), *Statistical correlation between economic activity and. Urban Systems*, 29:179–95

30   Ghosh, T., Anderson, S., Elvidge, C., and Sutton, P. (2013), *Using nighttime satellite imagery as a proxy measure of human well-being. Sustainability*, 5(12):4988–5019.

31 Sutton, P. C., Elvidge, C. D., & Ghosh, T. (2007), *Estimation of gross domestic product at sub-national scales using nighttime satellite imagery*, International Journal of Ecological Economics & Statistics, *8*(S07), 5-21.

32 Ebener, S., Murray, C., Tandon, A., Elvidge, C. C. (2005), *From wealth to health: modelling the distribution of income per capita at the sub-national level using night-time light imagery*, International journal of health geographics, 4(1), 5.

33 See 30.

34 Pinkovskiy and Sala-i Martin, (2014), Pinkovskiy, M. and Sala-i Martin, X. (2014), *Lights, camera,... income!: Estimating poverty using national accounts, survey means, and lights*, Technical report, National Bureau of Economic Research.

35 Pinkovskiy and Sala-i Martin, (2016), *Lights, camera. . . income! Illuminating the national accounts-household surveys debate.* The Quarterly Journal of Economics, 131(2), pp.579-631.

36 Kuan, C.-M. and White, H. (1994), *Artificial neural networks: An econometric perspective*, Econometric reviews, 13(1):1–91.

37 Maasoumi, E., Khotanzed, A., Abaye, A. (1994), *Artificial neural networks for some macroeconomic series: a first report*, Econometric Reviews, *13*(1), 105-122.

38 Tkacz, G., & Hu, S. (1999), *Forecasting GDP growth using artificial neural networks* (No. 1999-3). Bank of Canada.

39 Feng, L. and Zhang, J. (2014), *Application of artificial neural networks in tendency forecasting of economic growth*, Economic Modelling, 40:76–80.

40 Sokolov-Mladenovi´c et al., (2016), *RD expenditure and economic growth: EU28 evidence for the period 2002–2012*, Economic research-Ekonomska istra˙zivanja, 29(1), pp.1005-1020.

MEDIA FORMS

41 Correal (2014), *In New York City, Sunday Night Is for Regulars*, (Oct. 17, *The New York Times*, https://www.nytimes.com/2014/10/19/nyregion/after-saturday-nigh t-a-bit-of-old-new-york-can-still-be-found.html); Straw, W. (2015), *Media and the urban night.* Articulo-Journal of Urban Research.

42 Dominique, K. (2013), *Les bas-fonds.histoire d'un imaginaire.* Paris, Le Seuil.

43 Straw, W. (1997), *Urban confidential: The lurid city of the 1950s.*

WINE AND BEAR

44 According to Measham, F. (2004), *The decline of ecstasy, the rise of 'binge' drinking and the persistence of pleasure*, (Probation Journal 51 (4): 316), the definition

of what actually constitutes binge drinking is disputed and wavers between measurable quantities, in current terms called 'units' or 'standard drinks,' to purely subjective accounts such as drinking to the point of inebriation. Binge drinking has also come to be a loosely applied umbrella term to characterize any form of late-night anti-social behaviour in urban centres. Rather than quantifying an individual's blood alcohol content, or measuring how many units they have consumed, bingeing can be used to refer simply to any behaviour involving alcohol that is perceived to be rowdy or threatening (Hobbs, D. (2005) *Gluttony: 'Binge Drinking' and the Binge Economy. Economic and Social Research Council.* www.esrc.ac.uk/ESRCInfoCentre/about/CI/CP/research_publications/seven_sins/gluttony/index.aspx?ComponentId=10890&SourcePageId=11077). See *In: Planning the Night-time City* by Marion Roberts and Adam Eldridge, (2009), Routledge.

LATE-NIGHT

45 Barr, A. (1998), *Drink: a social history*, Pimlico.

46 Schivelbusch, W. (1988), *Disenchanted night: The industrialization of light in the nineteenth century*, trans. Angela Davies (Berkeley: University of California Press, 1988).

47 Amin, A., & Thrift, N. (2002), *Cities: reimagining the urban.* Polity Press.

48 Jayne, M., Valentine, G., and Holloway, S. L. (2008), *The place of drink: Geographical contributions to alcohol studies.*

MAPS

49 Boyce, P. R. (2019), *The benefits of light at night*, Building and Environment, 151, 356-367.

50 Jayne, M., Valentine, G., & Holloway, S. L. (2008), *The place of drink: Geographical contributions to alcohol studies.*

51 Earth's City Lights, available at *https://earthobservatory. nasa. gov/features/Lights.*

CULTURE

52 Lovatt, A. and O'Connor, J.(1995), *Cities and the night-time economy.* Planning Practice Research, 10(2):127–134.

TRANSPORT

53 McArthur, J., Robin, E., and Smeds, E. (2019), *Socio-spatial and temporal dimensions of transport equity for London's night time economy.* Transportation Research Part A: Policy and Practice, 121:433–443.

54 Rein, M., Schön, D., 2012. Frame-reflective policy discourse. *In:* Wagner, P., Weiss, C., Wittrock, B., Wollman, H. (Eds.), *Social Sciences and Modern States: National Experiences and Theoretical Crossroads.* Cambridge University Press, Berlin, pp. 262–289; Van Hulst, M., & Yanow, D. (2016). From policy "frames" to "framing" theorizing a more dynamic, political approach. *The American Review of Public Administration, 46*(1), 92-112.; Jorgensen, M. B. (2012). The diverging logics of integration policy making at national and city level. *International Migration Review, 46*(1), 244-278.

55

McArthur, J., Robin, E., & Smeds, E. (2019). Sociospatial and temporal dimensions of transport equity for London's night time economy. *Transportation Research Part A: Policy and Practice, 121,* 433-443, Chicago.

Plyushteva, A., & Boussauw, K. (2020). Does night-time public transport contribute to inclusive night mobility? Exploring Sofia's night bus network from a gender perspective. *Transport policy, 87.*

THE CITY THAT NEVER SLEEPS

56 Dan Q. Dao, (2019), *The Absolute Best Nightclubs And Lounges In New York City, Forbes (05/21)*, (Available at https://www.forbes.com/sites/dandao/2019/05/21/the-absolute-best-nightclubs-and-lounges-in-new-york-city/#7836663821f1).

57 Ackroyd, P. (2001), *London: The Biography.* London: Vintage.

58 A young man who behaves in an unpleasant or violent way as a result of excessive drinking.

59 In British English slang, Hooray Henry or Hoorah Henry (plural: Hoorah/*Hooray Henrys*/Henries) is a pejorative term, comparable to "toff", for an upper class British male who exudes loud-mouthed arrogance and an air of superiority, often flaunting his public school upbringing.

60 Ramsay, M. (1990), *Lagerland Lost? An Experiment in Keeping Drinkers off the Streets in Central Coventry and Elsewhere,* London: Home Office, Crime Prevention Unit.

MOST FASHIONABLE CITY

61 Perulli, P. (2020), *Milan in the age of global contract.* Glocalism. Five years of culture, politics and innovation-e-Book, 39.

BACK TO THE FEATURES

62 Hobbs, D., Lister, S., Hadfield, P., Winlow, S., and Hall, S. (2000). *Receiving shadows: governance and liminality in the night-time economy.* The British Journal of Sociology,

51(4):701-717.

REGULATION

63   Available at https://data.london.gov.uk/dataset/london-night-time-economy and https://www.lordmayors.org/?p=636

MUNICIPAL POLICY

64   **Boosterism** - is the act of promoting ("boosting") a town, city, or organization, with the goal of improving public perception of it. Boosting can be as simple as talking up the entity at a party or as elaborate as establishing a visitors' bureau. It has been somewhat associated with American small towns.

65   *Boosterism* is the act of promoting ("boosting") a town, city, or organization, with the goal of improving public perception of it. Boosting can be as simple as talking up the entity at a party or as elaborate as establishing a visitors' bureau. It has been somewhat associated with American small towns. Boosting is also done in political settings, especially in regard to disputed policies or controversial events.

66   Hadfield, P., Lister, S., Hobbs, D., (2001), *The '24-hour city' - condition critical*, Town Country Plan.

67   Hobbs, D., Winlow, S., Hadfield, P., & Lister, S. (2005). *Violent hypocrisy: Governance and the night-time economy*. European journal of criminology, 2(2), 161-183.

68   Hope, T . J. (1985,) *Drinking and disorder in the city: a policy analysis*, in: T. J. Hope, Implementing Crime Prevention Measures, Home Office Research Study No. 86 (London, HMSO), Tuck, M. (1989), *Drinking and Disorder: A Study of NonMetropolitan Violence*, Home Officer Research Study No. 108 (London, HMSO).

69   The logic of Keynesian interventionism in stimulating demand is that greater consumption causes a greater production of goods, greater employment and growth. But capitalism prospers, not if production rises, but if profitability rises. Production only increases if profitability rises and if there is a demand for the extra output—that is if a surplus-value can be both produced and realized (*in: International socialism, Radical economics, Marxist economics and Marx's economics, Issue:149, Posted on 6th January 2016*, Jane Hardy).

70   Keat, R., & Abercrombie, N. (Eds.). (1991), *Enterprise culture*. Routledge.

71   Hubbard, P., & Hall, T. (1998), *The entrepreneurial city and the 'new urban politics'. The entrepreneurial city: Geographies of politics, regime and representation*, 1-23; Hobbs, D., Hadfield, P., Lister, S., & Winlow, S. (2003), *Bouncers: Violence and governance in the night-time economy*. Oxford University Press on Demand.

72   Dick Hobbs, Philip Hadfield, Stuart Lister, and Simon Winlow, (2005), *Bouncers:*

Violence and Governance in the Night-Time Economy, ISBN-13: 9780199288007; Jessop, B. (1998). *The narrative of enterprise and the enterprise of narrative: place marketing and the entrepreneurial city*, The entrepreneurial city: Geographies of politics, regime and representation, 77-99.

73   Taylor, I. (1999), *Crime in context: a critical criminology of market societies*, London: Polity Press, p.131.

74   See Walsh, (2015), *Strengthening family resilience.* Guilford publications.

75   See 60, p.103.

76   Montgomery, J. (1990), *Cities and the art of cultural planning*, Planning Practice and research, 5(3), 17-24.

About the Author

Sergey Avetisyan is an economist and writer born and raised in Talin Armenia. Avetisyan's research interests lie in the field of urban economics, economic geography, and financial stability of the banking sector. Avetisyan is a Researcher at the Central Bank Of Armenia (CBA) in the Economic Research Department. He teaches urban and economic theory at Brusov State University.

You can connect with me on:
🐦 https://twitter.com/sergejavetisyan
📘 https://www.facebook.com/avetisyansergeyauthor